Answer the Question

The secret of exam success

Christopher Moor
MA (Cantab) MA Education (London) BA (London)
Vice-Principal ~~College~~ College of Further Education

NATIONAL EXTENSION COLLEGE
Course No. ED 13

If you **are** buying **Answer the Question** on its own you can still enrol as a correspondence student and enjoy the guidance of an experienced tutor. For details write to the National Extension College, 18 Brooklands Avenue, Cambridge CB2 2HN explaining that you have this book.

Acknowledgements

Many people have helped me to write this book. I should like to thank them all. First, my students; they acted as guinea-pigs for many of the ideas described. Next, my colleagues at Harrow College of Further Education: I picked their brains on many occasions, both over method of answering questions and over subject matter. And finally, Mr George Campbell, who constantly emphasised that the effort to express oneself clearly helps one to think clearly, and that the effort to think clearly helps one to express oneself clearly.

The National Extension College
18 Brooklands Avenue, Cambridge CB2 2HN
© National Extension College Trust Ltd. 1981
Reprinted 1985, 1986.
ISBN 0 86082 162 5

Design: Cover   David Cutting Graphics
              Text   Peter Hall
Photographs: John Walmsley
Printed by NEC Print

Contents

Preface

This book has been written to help the many examination candidates to whom the following comment all too often applies:

'The Board requires. . .some relevant information and some ability to handle it and to present a case. No amount of sociological or other jargon, just wandering on page after page, is an acceptable substitute. It is quite possible that if many candidates had less information, or less sophisticated information, and more skill in presenting their knowledge and ideas, they would have received higher marks.'*

The book shows how to acquire skill in presentation and hence how to gain higher marks. Now it must be remembered that the subject of presentation is a difficult one: different teachers and different examiners have different ideas about it. The advice in the pages that follow is given with the full knowledge that it concerns a delicate subject 'where angels fear to tread.' Because of this, reasons are given as far as possible for whatever is suggested.

You may decide *not* to follow the advice given. Even so, the book may help you to find your own solution to problems by first making you aware of them and then analysing them.

Introduction

How to use this book

This book is rather more than just a text-book: at intervals you are invited to pause and reflect on what you have read. You are, in fact, asked self-assessment questions, in order to test your understanding of the subject matter. When you come across these questions, do your best to answer them. Cover up the answers in the text until you have jotted down your own answers on a piece of paper.

Then compare your jottings with each given answer. The two need not be identical, but if they are wildly adrift you have probably not understood what you have read. In that event re-read it straightaway. Only if you are sure you understand what has gone before, should you read on.

Assignments

At the end of some units, assignments are set. If you are following a correspondence course, you should write your answers to each assignment and send them off to your tutor before starting to study the next chapter. Follow the instructions at the beginning of each assignment carefully, particularly with regard to the time to be taken.

Make as much use of your tutor as you can. If you have any queries, write them at the bottom of the script you send to him.

If you are not a correspondence student, but are studying the course by yourself, there is little point in attempting the assignments unless you have someone to correct them. But you should still answer the self-assessment questions.

If you are following the course as a member of a class your teacher may decide to set you assignments appropriate to the particular subject you are studying. In this case you will obviously answer his assignments rather than the ones in the text.

Another point should be made at this stage: to help you find your way about this book, different type faces have been used. The main body of the book is set in normal 'Medium' type. **Self assessment questions and assignments are set in a 'Bold' type face;** *discussion of such questions is in italics.* So, if you want to look for particular points in the text, look for them in Medium type; if you want to question yourself on these points look for Bold type; if you want to see these questions discussed, look for italics.

At the beginning of each unit, the main points are summarised. A box has been left beside each point for you to note down the number of the page on which the point is made. Enter these numbers when you have finished each chapter. The act of searching out the points and making a note will help impress the points on your memory.

And now, without further ado, Good Reading; work hard!

4

1.General Problems

Summary

In this unit we cover the following points:
(The student is recommended to insert the page number as an aid to revision)   *Page*

This book is designed, not to teach you your subject matter, but to show you how to answer questions which involve making a reasoned judgement.   — — —

You should define all abstract terms used. (More about this in Unit 2).   — — —

You should allow yourself a wide enough scope to encompass all important points, but not so wide as to become irrelevant.   — — —

Your intention should be to persuade the examiner of the reasonableness of your view. (More about this in Unit 3.)   — — —

Build your case upon the examiner's knowledge. Remind him of facts. Do not try to startle him with brilliant new ideas! Make yourself crystal clear.   — — —

Do not intrude your own opinions too strongly.   — — —

There are two views about where your own opinions should be stated: in the 'jury method', it should be at the end (like a verdict); in the 'advocate method', it should go at the beginning.   — — —

1.1 Introduction

This book is aimed at helping you to answer questions of a particular type — those in which you are asked to make a judgement. Such questions crop up in a wide range of examinations. You meet a few at O-level, and many more at A-level and degree standard. They are especially common in the arts and social sciences. They frequently take the form of a quotation which you are asked to discuss. For instance, from a History paper:

> 'A hollow triumph.' Do you agree with this judgement of the Treaty of Troyes, 1420?

or from an English Literature paper:

> 'The slap-stick comedy scenes spoil the play.' Consider this comment on *The Tempest*.

or from a paper on Law:

'An acceptance in law involves an unconditional assent to the terms of the offer.' Discuss.

or from a paper on Biology:

'The bryophytes and amphibians are of little interest or importance to any except biologists.' Discuss this view of these two groups of organisms.

These four questions, though from different fields of learning, have a similar form. In each, the examiner has chosen a statement about the subject you have studied; he has asked you to comment on the statement in the light of your knowledge. Each statement has more than a grain of truth in it, but each is quoted out of context. For all you know, the author of each quotation went on to modify it to some extent. Whether he did or not, each quotation by itself is at best a half-truth. It needs to be set in a new context – to be re-assessed. Put into typical examiner's language, each needs to be 'discussed' or 'considered'.

Let us look a little more deeply at a question from an A-level English paper:

To what extent does the structure of *To The Lighthouse* contribute to the success of the novel?

To answer such a question, you must have studied the novel carefully, you must know the plot, you must understand the characters, and you must be familiar – either from listening to your teacher or from your reading about Virginia Woolf – with the main points of discussion about the book. And in some way, your answer must reflect your knowledge.

But the question involves two other elements which you must come to grips with. First, there is the abstract term 'structure'. What does this mean? What is the structure of *To the Lighthouse?* You must ask and answer questions of this sort.

Secondly, you are asked to make a judgement: *To what extent* does structure contribute to success? Is structure very important or is it only of secondary importance? Your answer must give an indication of your view.

Now, many A-level and university degree questions, in many different subjects are of this sort. They involve abstract terms which need definition and explanation. They also involve judgement. When students first meet this type of question, they tend to feel lost. It is not obvious to them how to use the material they have learned in such a way as to give a good account of themselves.

Which brings us to the purpose of this book. First, it must be made clear that this book is *not* designed to teach you your subject matter. It is assumed that you have access to, and are capable of understanding and learning, both the primary material – the main facts about the subject – and the secondary material – the main arguments used by scholars, critics and commentators in discussing the primary material. This book, on the other hand, is designed to help you, when you know your subject, to marshal your ideas so as to use them convincingly. In other words, this book should help you to use your knowledge so as to give a reasoned judgement.

Let us now look at certain general points which you should be aware of when answering examination questions of the type under discussion.

1.2. Definitions

There is first the problem of defining abstract terms. Let us take an example from an A-level Sociology paper:

'We are all middle-class now.' Discuss.

You are evidently expected to make some sort of judgement about whether or not we are all middle-class. But how can you do that without a clear idea of the meaning of the term? And this is the difficulty. There are many different meanings to 'middle-class.' Some have to do with your income, some with your education, some with your speech, some with your image of yourself, and some with other people's image of you. Whether or not you can say that we are all middle-class thus depends upon the way in which you define the term. Your answer must explain this, and it is hardly surprising therefore that a considerable portion of it will be devoted to making clear just exactly what you are taking 'middle-class' to mean.

Self Assessment Question
You may know nothing at all about the topics below. You have probably never heard of *Nasi Furianti* nor of Lin Tse-hsu! But that will not prevent you from dealing satisfactorily with the self assessment questions which follow. In fact you should beware lest any knowledge you may possess of the topics leads you away from the point. With that warning, here is the question:

Of the following examination questions, which four is this book primarily designed to help you to answer?

1 **'Induction plays no part in scientific method.' Evaluate this claim. (Logic)**

2 **Give an outline of the early history of the Trade Union Movement in England. (History)**

3 **Despite its apparent simplicity, *Nasi Furianti* is one of the main pioneering works of Czech drama. Do you agree? (Drama)**

4 **What is the dramatic function of the witches in *Macbeth?* (English Literature)**

5 **'Multi-programming techniques have revolutionalised computer applications.' Discuss (Computer Studies)**

6 **Evaluate the role of Lin Tse-hsu in precipitating the first Anglo-Chinese war. (Chinese History)**

Discussion

This book should help you to answer 1, 3, 5 and 6. In each of these questions you are asked to make a judgement: words like 'evaluate' and 'discuss' are clues. So, as we shall show shortly, is the question 'Do you agree?'

As for question 2 on the history of the Trade Union Movement, and 4 on the dramatic function of the witches, neither of these is directly dealt with in the book. You are not asked to make a judgement in them, but only to outline or describe.

Self-Assessment Questions

What abstract concepts must you come to grips with (by defining or explaining them) in answering each of the following questions?

Again, no knowledge of specific topics — *Kongens Fald*, *Volpone*, de Gaulle and so on — is required to answer this self-assessment question. You are not asked 'to come to grips with' the abstract concepts but only to state what these abstract concepts are.

1 **'*Kongens Fald* is a novel about national and personal degradation.' Discuss (Danish Literature)**

2 **Do you agree that the comedy in *Volpone* is more cruel than amusing? (English Literature)**

3 **How far did de Gaulle, as President of the Fifth Republic, fulfil the expectations of his supporters? (History)**

4 **'Language is not a matter of instinct, but a matter of convention.' Do you agree (English)**

5 **How far is Dobbin the hero of *Vanity Fair?* (English Literature)**

6 **Discuss the extent to which growth in living organisms is controlled by the action of hormones. (Biology)**

Discussion

1 'Kongens Fald is a novel about national and personal degradation.' Discuss (Danish Literature)

To answer this question, you must explain what you take 'degradation' to mean. You must distinguish too between national degradation and personal degradation. These are key concepts: without getting to grips with them you cannot answer the question, however thoroughly you may know Kongens Fald.

2 Do you agree that the comedy in Volpone is more cruel than amusing? (English Literature)

Here you must consider what is meant by 'cruel comedy' as opposed to 'amusing comedy.' If the comedy is cruel, who is being hurt? If only amusing, is there any *serious comment which Ben Jonson is making about human nature? You obviously will not get far without knowing Volpone, but even if you know it well, your answer will be unsatisfactory without a clearly thought-out discussion about relevant aspects of comedy.*

3 How far did de Gaulle, as President of the Fifth Republic, fulfil the expectations of his supporters? (History)

This time you must make clear just what you think 'the expectations of his supporters' were. Now, many candidates would have described in detail de Gaulle's achievements, and they might have described them perfectly. But that was not what they were asked to do! They would get poor marks in consequence for an irrelevant answer.

Somehow, in a question of this sort, you must use your knowledge of de Gaulle's achievements and of what his supporters expected him to achieve, in order to make a judgement. How far did he fulfil their expectations? Entirely? Not at all? OR somewhere in between? That is for you to judge.

4 'Language is not a matter of instinct but a matter of convention' Do you agree? (English)

In this question you will need to pay attention to what is meant by 'instinct' on the one hand and by 'convention' on the other.

5 How far is Dobbin the hero of Vanity Fair? (English Literature)

This time, the precise meaning of 'hero' is crucial.

6 Discuss the extent to which growth in living organisms is controlled by the action of hormones. (Biology)

Here, you must concentrate on the idea of growth being 'controlled' by hormones, rather than just influenced by them. Are there other things which influence growth — the genes, the environment, perhaps? If so, which of these factors is the dominant one? Without examining such ideas, no amount of knowledge about the hormones themselves will make your answer adequate.

1.3 Scope

Linked with the problem of definition of terms is the problem of how narrowly you should stick to your subject. How wide a scope are you allowed? Should you keep rigidly to the point or should you roam far and wide, drawing in examples from many fields, however remote? One must presumably take some sort of middle course, avoiding both extremes. For example, if answering a question concerning the relative importance of theme and plot in *The Tempest*, one should not deal with characterisation, imagery and diction. This would be to wander off into irrelevance. One must stick more or less to theme and plot. But what is the theme of *The Tempest?* Is there more than one theme? If so, which is the dominant one? There is plenty of room here for exploration.

Perhaps we can generalise by saying that one needs to roam over the field widely enough to encompass all important points. But one must keep one's eye on the main goal. And after dealing in detail with an example, one would be wise to return to the main line of the argument.

1.4   Persuasion

The two problems outlined above concern the need for defining terms and the 'scope' of your answer. The third problem is absolutely central, and concerns the whole intention of your answer. In the type of question we are dealing with, in which judgement is required, your intention must be to persuade, not merely to inform. This is crucial. No amount of telling a story or explaining facts will convince someone of an argument. The two processes are not really related to one another.

Let us take an example from a History paper:

'A fine commander but a poor statesman.' Discuss this comment on King Alfred.

You must of course be familiar with the main facts about King Alfred's life and of the times in which he lived. But to tell his life story will just not do! No amount of detail about his battles and laws will even begin to get to the point. You are not asked to describe the battles he fought nor even the tactics he employed. You are asked about his qualities as a commander and as a statesman. You must therefore set out what qualities are required in both 'jobs', and assess the extent to which King Alfred possessed these qualities.

If you find yourself describing battles, beware! It is fairly safe to say that, if when answering a question where judgement is called for, you find yourself giving information or telling the story, you are on the wrong track. Stop at once and ask yourself 'Why am I telling the examiner this? Should I not be persuading him a line of argument instead?'

1.5   Your attitude towards the examiner

Which brings us to another crucial problem, namely your attitude towards the examiner. After all, you are not writing in a vacuum. What you write will be read by a particular person, the examiner, even if you do not know who he is. But are you writing *for* him?

Well, the brief answer to that question is 'No'! If you were capable of writing answers which would make the examiner sit up and take notice – introducing him to material he had never come across and suggesting ideas to him which had never passed through his mind – you would hardly be an examinee! Much more likely you would be a university professor, long embarked on a distinguished career of scholarship. As a student, however, you are unlikely to be able to answer the examiner on his level.

It is better to imagine yourself writing for someone on an academic level just below yours. For instance, if you are taking your A-level examinations, think that you are writing for a friend who has just passed O-level in your subject. Or if you are taking your final degree examinations, imagine that you are writing for a second-year student. In either case, there are a number of assumptions to be made about your reader which will enable you to pitch your answer at the right level.

To begin with, you can assume that your reader knows the subject matter as well as you: if you allude to a specific incident, he will know what you are referring to. You do not need to bore him by telling him the facts; instead, you can use his knowledge of those facts to support the point which you are making.

Next, you can assume that your reader has read most of the commentators and critics on the subject. (And if he hasn't, he ought to have done!) You are unlikely to be able to startle him with brilliant new ideas. So don't try to; you would be hard put to it to back them up with enough evidence to convince him of their reasonableness. By and large, you will be well advised to stick to familiar lines of argument.

On the other hand, your reader has no means of knowing what is in your mind unless you tell him. He may know what *he* means by a particular word or phrase, but the only way for him to know what *you* mean by it is for you to tell him. Hence the importance, which we will refer to later, of defining abstract terms.

The general point to bear in mind is that, as with any other form of communication, the examination answer is aimed at a particular reader. The more you consider the likely reactions and sensibilities of that reader, the more likely you are to make a favourable impact upon him.

The examiner's function is to judge whether, in his opinion, you have written convincingly for someone who knows the subject matter but who does not know your view of it. The examiner is trying to assess your ability to explain what you know, not so much to him as to the sort of people with whom you will spend your life. In this respect the examiner resembles a baked-bean taster whose job it is to judge, not whether he likes the baked beans, but whether the public will like them. Only the examiner is dealing with somewhat more lofty products than baked beans.

1.6 Your own opinions

We move on now to consider the extent to which your own opinions should be expressed. How far are your own views actually wanted by the examiner? Consider this question from a Sociology paper:

'The main function of apprenticeship is to regulate entry into the skilled professions.' Do you agree?

On the face of it, you might answer with a bare 'yes' and leave it at that! 'I was asked if I agreed,' you might say, 'and I said I did. I ought to get full marks.'

Unfortunately for you, that is too naive a view. The question 'Do you agree?' is a shorthand for 'give a reasoned judgement.' The examiner expects you to realize this. Your 'yes' would bring you no marks at all!

But suppose you say that you agree with the statement and then go on to give as many reasons as you can for agreeing. Would this not suffice?

Well, hardly.

The examiner is only partly interested in your views and opinions, even if you back them up. What he wants to know almost always is whether you can set out the arguments on *both* sides and weigh them up, one side against the other, whatever your own feelings may be. His job is to choose questions where there are points to make both for and against, and then to assess your ability to balance the arguments. Your opinions are of secondary importance to him.

1.7 Originality

One other point may be raised here. It concerns the question of whether you should follow the line you think your teacher has advocated, or whether you should strike out on your own and give a personal view-point. To put it another way, should you regurgitate the teacher's notes, on the assumption that he wants to read his own views; or should you give your own views in the belief that what matters most is your own 'original' assessment?

It is obviously rash to be dogmatic on this issue. One never knows for certain how an examiner's mind works! One can however say that merely to trot out opinions gleaned from your teacher is unlikely to be a good way of answering the question. For one thing, these opinions are worthless on their own: they need justifying. For another, they will almost certainly have been given in a slightly different context to that of the particular examination question: they are thus unlikely to be strictly relevant. Something more is required of you than that you should re-issue other people's views.

On the other hand, it is not very often that you have the chance of being original in the sense of finding a completely new angle on an issue. Unfortunately, the examiner will already have weighed up most of the important arguments on either side of the question; that is what qualifies him to be an examiner! What he is looking for is evidence that your knowledge and the opinions you have heard or read have all been thoroughly digested to form a coherent whole; that you have managed to synthesise the many different elements of the subject and are capable of dealing with conflicting views.

Of course, there are occasions when your personal views are important. This is especially the case when you answer questions which involve moral issues. For example, in answering the question:

How far are Ernest Pontifex's* parents responsible for his behaviour?

---

*Ernest Pontifex, the main character of Samuel Butler's *The Way of All Flesh*, suffered from an unhappy upbringing by repressive narrow-minded "Victorian" parents. The book describes Ernest's turbulent progress towards a mature adulthood.

your own view of 'responsibility' will colour your judgement. If you feel that each of us is responsible for his own behaviour, your answer to the question will be different from that of someone who feels that behaviour is largely conditioned by one's parents and upbringing. In answering the question, you will be wise to tell the examiner where you stand, as it were, in making your judgement – from what viewpoint you are looking at 'responsibility'.

But again, the examiner is particularly interested in seeing whether you can achieve your own synthesis of the subject matter and sometimes of conflicting interpretations of it, and it is in this sense that your answer should be original. If you have worked on your material in such a way that it has been totally assimilated into your mind, your answers will display a freshness and vitality even on well-trodden paths. They will show the kind of 'wit' to which Pope was referring to his 'Essay on Criticism:'

True wit is Nature to advantage dress'd:
What oft was thought, but ne'er so well expressed.

Self-Assessment Question
A student is answering the question:

Discuss Galileo's importance as a scientific discoverer.

Explain what is wrong with his use of the following paragraph in doing so:

Having heard that a Dutchman had lately invented a telescope, Galileo made one himself, and very quickly discovered a number of important things. He found that the Milky Way consists of a multitude of separate stars. He observed the phases of Venus, which Copernicus knew to be implied by his theory, but which the naked eye was unable to perceive. And he discovered the satellites of Jupiter.*

Discussion
What the student has done wrong is, quite simply, this: he has not ANSWERED THE QUESTION set. Instead, he has answered a different question: 'Describe some of Galileo's achievements.' And as he was not asked to do this, he will get few marks!

The question set asks for a judgement to be made: how important was Galileo as a scientific discoverer? Very important? Not at all important? Or somewhere in between? The student must make up his mind and answer accordingly.

And there is a key concept to be unravelled: what is meant by a 'scientific

---

(The paragraph quoted is taken from Bertrand Russell's History of Western Philosophy. The criticism of the student just given does not apply to Russell who was not answering an examination question! His purpose in writing was different – to describe to a layman what Galileo actually did.)

discoverer'? Is it someone who locks himself in a laboratory and fiddles around with new-fangled gadgets? Or someone who attempts to unlock the secrets of the universe? Whatever you take it to mean, you must tell the examiner. You can then use your knowledge of Galileo to place his achievements in context. You can allude to these achievements rather than describe them – the examiner should know them.

To summarise: the question about Galileo requires a judgement to be made about an abstract topic (what has been called above a 'Key Concept.')

Self-Assessment Questions
Make a judgement on each of the following questions and show how you would unravel the key concepts.

1 To what extent was Harold MacMillan a successful politician?

2 'History is bunk' (Henry Ford) Do you agree?

3 'Microprocessors will revolutionise society.' To what extent do you feel this prediction to be justified?

Discussion
Everyone will think differently about these subjects, but here are some possible lines of approach:

1 To what extent was Harold MacMillan a successful politician?
Judgement: Harold MacMillan was one of the most successful politicians of post-war years.
Unravelling the key concept: What is meant by a politician? Someone who persuades his supporters that he can provide the answers to their problems? Or someone who is far-sighted and resolute enough to set his country on the right course even if his fellow men disagree with his views?
Whether you agree with the judgement above will depend on which of these definitions of politician you feel is nearer the truth.

2 'History is bunk.' (Henry Ford) Do you agree?

Judgement: While it is probably true that history never repeats itself exactly, to say that 'history is bunk' is to take a too pessimistic view of the use we can make of the experience of the past.
Unravelling the key concept: What does the phrase mean? That the history books are untrue, in the sense that historians do not really know what happened in the past because they were not there? Or that even if we do know what happened, it will not help us to solve our own problems because the circumstances surrounding them are so different from those surrounding past problems?
Your judgement will vary according to what you take Henry Ford's

phrase to mean.

3 *'Microprocessors will revolutionise society.' To what extent do you feel this prediction to be justified?*

> *Judgement: To say that microprocessors will revolutionise society is to exaggerate both the likely change and the speed with which those changes will be brought about.*
>
> *Unravelling the key concepts: What does 'to revolutionise society' mean? To change society to a considerable extent? Or to change it so fast that the whole structure breaks down in a violent manner?*
>
> *What changes will microprocessors bring about? Changes to production methods only, or to the ways in which we relate to other people (with truth, honesty, justice) as well?*
>
> *Will we be adaptable enough to cope with the pace of change, or will it overwhelm us?*
>
> *Depending on your answers to such self-questioning, so your judgement will vary from the judgement given above.*

2. Analysis of the question

... leaving one still with the intolerable wrestle. With words and meanings
T S Eliot

Summary

In this Unit the following points are made:
(The student is recommended to insert the page numbers as an aid   *Page*
to revision)

Analyse the question thoroughly: — — —

   What do the various abstract terms mean?
   What does each phrase mean?
   What does the question as a whole mean?

Tell the examiner what you take the question to mean.   — — —

Analyse in depth. Do not allow yourself to give up too soon.   — — —

Your analysis is the foundation upon which your answer will be built.

2.1 Introduction

In subjects where abstract terms are employed, it is vital that you analyse the
question thoroughly. You must ask yourself 'What does the question mean?
What do the various abstract terms mean? Can I define them? Am I tackling the
whole question or just a part of it?' And so on.

Too many candidates fail to answer the questions set, or substitute questions
of their own and write accordingly! Others read only half the question, ignoring
important aspects of the argument in consequence. Only by a methodical
analysis of the question will you avoid these pitfalls.

2.2 What does the question mean?

Consider this question from an A-level English paper:

'Mr Yeats starts in the English tradition, but he is from the outset an Irish
poet.' Discuss.

You may very well conclude that the quotation means that although Yeats
wrote to begin with in traditional English verse forms, the feeling expressed
through his poetry was that of an Irishman. But how can you be sure? Faced
with the sort of question above, you must start asking yourself a whole range of
analytical questions, including for example:

17

1 What is 'the English tradition?' Does the phrase have any meaning? If so, can I define it? Is it some quality or qualities which all English poets share? If so, what qualities are these? Are they to do with theme, with content, with style or with something else?

2 What is an Irish poet? Is it something political? or is it to do with the quality of Irish life? Or writers?

3 What is the difference between *to start in* (the English tradition) and *to be from the outset* (an Irish poet)? Is one something learned and the other something inherited? And if so, which is which?

It is useful to jot these kinds of questions down, because it is from your answers to them that you will be able to build up your essay. If you have asked significant questions, then the answer to each will very likely give you material for a paragraph directly relevant to the question asked.

To illustrate rather more fully the need for careful analysis, let us look at another question, this time from a History paper:

'Richard II failed because he took too many calculated risks.' Do you agree?

First, it is fairly obvious that Richard failed: he was after all imprisoned by Bolingbroke and eventually murdered. Even so, it is perhaps worth thinking briefly about whether he failed *completely*. Think whether he had any achievements which survived his death, bearing in mind that his was the court in which Chaucer flourished, that he provided the inspiration for Shakespeare's play, and that his usurper was at considerable pains to suppress his memory. It may be that these issues signify little in comparison with others you consider relevant. The point is that you should not assume that they are insignificant without at least considering them.

Probably, in the Richard II statement, you will feel that the crux lies in the phrase 'too many calculated risks.' What is a calculated risk? Is it one in which you weigh up the chances of success and failure, but rely too much on luck? Or is it one in which you feel that the stakes are so high that you choose a course of action which in other circumstances you would not choose? Or is it something different from either of these? And, whatever a calculated risk is, how many of them can you take with impunity? One? Or none at all?

Posing yourself questions of this kind will help you to clarify in your own mind just what it means to take 'too many calculated risks.' Only then will you be in a position to sift through the evidence in order to judge whether or not Richard took too many.

2.3 Explaining your interpretation of the question

Having staked out for yourself, then, what you think the question means, you must explain your ideas to the examiner. Let us take the following question from an A-level English paper as an example:

'Political and social propaganda in the theatre, as a general rule, is a cracking bore.' Is this true of Shaw's *Major Barbara?**

Now let us suppose that you feel *Major Barbara* to have a fair measure of social message in it, but that you do not find it 'a cracking bore.' How are you to reconcile this apparent contradiction and present a convincing case to the examiner?

Well, you must analyse the quotation by asking yourself a range of questions, such as: What is propaganda? How do I define it? Is it an attempt to convert someone to a particular framework of beliefs? Do propagandists mind whether they bore you or not, provided they achieve their results? Do people go to the theatre to be 'converted' or to be entertained? In what ways do the methods of playwrights differ from those of propagandists? To what emotions do both kinds of writer appeal? Could I say that a playwright appeals more to the heart and a propagandist more to the head? Or is that an oversimplification?

All these questions are very general, and on the face of it seem to have nothing to do with Shaw, and still less with *Major Barbara*. They must however be answered in order that you can get on to the problem of how Shaw managed to make *Major Barbara* a lively play full of tension, excitement, humour and social and political comment without boring his audience.

Your answer will therefore need some such paragraph as the following, before you can get down to writing about the play itself:

It is true that the theatre is not a suitable place for social and political propaganda. One pays to be entertained, not to be converted to someone else's philosophy. Or at any rate, if one is to be converted, it must be by much more subtle means than those of the propagandist, whose method is often to maintain an assault on his listener's intelligence. For he will constantly repeat himself, make frequent use of slogans, and stir up in his listener admiration for a particular person or type of person, and hatred for another. He tends to see things in black and white, and he is usually devoid of humour. Unlike the dramatist, he is not interested in the rich variety of human life, and his purpose is hardly to entertain.

Of course, this is a personal opinion and it would be as well to acknowledge the fact. But a paragraph of this sort will give a lead in to show how Shaw, though intent on making social and political points, managed to avoid the propagandist's methods. It will give you a firm foundation on which to build your answer. You

---

*Barbara Undershaft, a Major in the Salvation Army, is convinced that she can save the souls of her down-and-out clients in an East End shelter. She is finally converted to a very different faith after seeing the armaments factory and model town owned and managed by her father, Andrew Undershaft.

can consider the human interest of Shaw's play, the emotions aroused by it, the use of paradox and humour, and the succession of tensions and their resolutions which go to make up the plot — all the features, in fact, which make the play good theatre and prevent it becoming 'a cracking bore.' The superstructure of your answer, in other words, will have been built upon the foundations of your introductory analysis of the question.

2.4 Definition of abstract and technical terms

Now, just as part of this analysis may involve setting out your interpretation of the question in broad terms, so part of it may be to define abstract and technical terms in some considerable detail. You should never assume, for instance, that meanings of such terms as 'realism', 'romantic,' 'humanitarian' or 'utilitarian' are self-evident. Each of them has been used time and again by different writers, and each writer has used them with somewhat different connotations. So you should define abstract terms closely every time you use them. Do not assume, either, just because the examiner has used some term in a question, that its meaning can be taken for granted. The examiner wants to test your ability to handle such terms, and handling them involves defining them.

Often, to 'define' terms means to make them more precise. In a question, for example, on the causes of the French Revolution, it is obvious what is meant *approximately* by 'French Revolution'. It is still necessary to establish the *precise* meaning of the term. You have been asked the cause of some event; you must say exactly what you take that event to be and when it took place. Only then can you work backwards to give the causes of it. Did the French Revolution begin when the Third Estate resolved that no tax should be levied without its consent? Or did it begin with the storming of the Bastille on July 14 1789? Or with the 'orgy' of August 4? Depending on your definition, your account of the causes of the Revolution will vary.

In the example just given, a term has been defined by looking more closely at it. Another method of definition is to say what the concept under discussion is like, and what it is *not* like. Suppose you are discussing the dramatic quality of some of John Donne's poetry. You must define in what sense you are using the term 'dramatic.' You might decide therefore to say that

Donne's poetry is frequently dramatic, in the sense, not that it could be presented on stage, but that conflict is inherent in it.

You would probably go on to give an example so as to make your definition totally clear:

In *The Flea,* for instance, the poet addresses his would-be mistress, attempting to overcome her resistance to sleeping with him. The poem could not be *acted* because only the poet's 'lines' are presented. But the lady's part is implied: each of her possible arguments is countered. Conflicting views are thus set forth in the poem, conflict being of course an essential quality of drama.

By giving examples of what you include in your definition of a concept — and what you exclude — you will make it more precise. The sort of formulae, therefore, which are useful in defining terms are:

In this context, the term T means . . .
It is X in the sense that it is more like Y than like Z.
By P, we imply that it is like Q not R.

You may find it helpful to use some such formula whenever you introduce a term whose meaning is in any way vague or ambiguous.

A small point is worth making here. Do not think there is some 'right' definition of any abstract term. Do not think you must, for example, use the dictionary definition. Over and above what any term 'denotes', it has a range of associated meanings — its 'connotations' which, taken altogether, make up its 'semantic field'. Abstract terms tend to have a wide semantic field.

What matters is that you tell the examiner what *you* mean when you use a word: provided your choice lies reasonably within the semantic field, and that you have located it accurately, you are entitled to choose more or less as you like.

Now it is not merely those terms which one might call difficult that need definition — the -isms, -ilities, -arians, -ocracies and so on. Sometimes quite simple terms require attention. You should look for the 'key' words and define these. A question for an M.A. paper in Education illustrates this:

Is it true that the education service is a partnership between central government and local education authorities?

Here the key word is 'partnership.' Your answer to the question will vary according to the meaning you place on this word. Does 'partnership' here involve equals or can you have senior and junior partners? Is it equally open to each member of a partnership to propose, legislate, refuse to act, take the initiative, comply with, coerce? These are the kinds of questions you must consider before you can decide upon your answer.

Your questioning will not merely lead you to make the required judgement as to the truth of the statement; you can use each element of your questioning as a probe, to examine the relationship between central government and local authorities. You could, for example, ask whether the term 'partner' is appropriate in the case where one so-called partner can, by legislation, create the other. Your answer might involve discussion of Local Government Acts because these would throw light on the relationship between central and local government. Or you could ask whether, in a legal tussle, central government always wins. Your answer here might deal with recent cases over comprehensive reorganisation where judgement was given *against* the Secretary of State and in favour of a local authority. This, too, throws light on the relationship. The questions you ask, even about the meanings of quite common words, will often help you to frame your answer.

On the other hand, you should not waste time defining what is fairly obviously common ground between you and the examiner. If asked, for instance, 'To what extent, can Britain be described as a meritocracy?' do not spend time defining 'Britain'! What needs your attention is the word 'meritocracy'. You can afford to take 'Britain' for granted.

To put the point more generally: it is vitally important to analyse the question and this will often entail defining certain key words. Don't assume that the examiner will know what *you* mean by some expression even if *he* has used it in his question. Define the terms you use; in other words, explore their connotations, showing which meanings you accept and which you reject for the purpose of your answer.

The section of your essay in which you perform this analysis will act as a foundation upon which to build your case. Your knowledge of your subject, which you will later display, will then show up clearly and will be seen to be relevant to the question you are answering.

2.5 The need for thorough analysis

One last point: we are most of us lazy! Posing questions and answering them is hard work; one tends to give up easily. But without thorough probing – really getting down to the roots of the question – one's answers will be at best superficial and at worst irrelevant. So don't give up! When you run out of questions, force yourself to ask 'Is there anything else – anything I have overlooked?' There almost certainly will be. Go on squeezing your brain till you have wrung the last idea out of it.

Self-Assessment Questions

Analyse what seem to be the key words or concepts in each of the following essay topics. In other words, jot down significant questions you would ask about each.

1 Do animals have rights?

2 Does Churchill deserve his reputation?

3 'The exception proves the rule'. Discuss.

4 'Manners makyth man.' Discuss.

5 'I never consider a poem great if I can understand it.' How far would you take this statement seriously?

Discussion

Everyone will ask different questions about each of these topics, but here are some which you might ask:

1 Do animals have rights?

What do we mean by rights? What kind of rights can animals have? The right to live? If so, how can we justify killing them? The right to be free? If so, how do we justify caging them? The right to have some purpose independent of man? If so, how do we justify their use in experiments for the benefit of man?

Are any rights they may have absolute rights? If not, who gives the rights? And who can take them away? Do some animals have more rights than others? Or are there some rights which all animals (including man) should enjoy?

2 Does Churchill deserve his reputation?

What is someone's 'reputation'? What his friends say about him? Or what his enemies say? Or what some objective observer says? Can there be such a person anyway? Are people emotionally biased when they talk about Churchill?

What do you take Churchill's reputation to be? Does he deserve this reputation? Or does it omit certain qualities? Or over-emphasise others? Should he have some different reputation? If so, what should it be?

3 'The exception proves the rule.' Discuss.

What are rules and how are they derived? What kinds of rules are there? Are some more absolute than others? Are there any 'natural' rules? What about rules made by governments? And school rules? What have they in common? Are they generalisations of some basic principles? If so, perhaps they never apply strictly. Or do they?

What does it mean, to 'prove' a rule? Should 'prove' really be 'test' or 'try?' Then the statement could read 'The exception tests the rule' (to see whether or not it holds). But is this how ordinary people interpret the statement? Or do they take it literally?

4 'Manners makyth man.' Discuss.

What does this mean? That 'manners' are what distinguish men from animals? And are 'manners' just table manners and the like? Or customs? If so, what customs? All? Or just the good ones?

What actually 'makes man'? What actually distinguishes him from animals? His reason? If so, why do men appear to use their reason to harm other men?

Is the quotation perhaps referring to some ideal of what man should be? With certain praise-worthy qualities? If so, what qualities? Are these derived from the ideal man's respect for the feelings of others? Is this respect the basis of 'manners'?

5 'I never consider a poem great if I can understand it.' How far would you take this statement seriously?

What makes a poem great? Is it the technical skill of the writer? Or the feeling expressed in the poem? Or the way the writer has used his technical skill to express significant human feelings?

And what is involved in 'understanding' a poem? Can one appreciate it without fully understanding it? Does this mean almost by definition that if something is too easily understood at first it cannot be great? Is there some virtue in obscurity? Were some great poems obscure when they were first written but have now become less so? Perhaps because the poems have grown familiar to us?

These are obviously not all the questions you could ask about the essay topics, and you may feel that they are not all relevant. They are meant to illustrate, however, the sort of way in which you should be working — asking yourself questions and jotting them down. You will then have some ideas on paper in front of you when you come to write your answer.

Assignment A

Choose one of the topics in the Self Assessment section on page 21 and write an answer to it in not more than 500 words.

You may find the list of questions asked in the Discussion Section helpful and you may want to add questions of your own to it. Think of as many extra ones as possible.

When you are ready to write your answer, limit yourself to one hour for the actual writing.

Send your tutor:

(a)   Your answer, with a note of the exact time taken, and

(b)   A list of the questions you thought of.

The most important part of this assignment is the analysis you are able to make of the topic set. Do not be afraid that you are stating the obvious or making too elementary points. It is a fault on the right side. Most students seem to assume that the examiner is a professional mind-reader. He is not!

In this unit we have discussed the need for a thorough analysis of the question. In the next we shall consider the structure and function of the individual paragraphs which you will use to construct your answer.

3.Paragraphs

> .....And every phrase
> And sentence that is right (where every word is at home,
> Taking its place to support the others,
> The word neither diffident not ostentatious,
> An easy commerce of the old and the new,
> The common word exact without vulgarity,
> The formal word precise but not pedantic,
> The complete consort dancing together)
> Every phrase and every sentence is an end and a beginning.
>
> T S Eliot

Summary
In this unit the following points are made: (students are recommended to fill in the page numbers as an aid to revision)   *Page*

Structure of paragraphs

1 Paragraphs are governed by a controlling idea   — — —

   — what the paragraph is about
   — the main point being made
   — what unifies the paragraph

2 They contain the *topic sentence*   — — —

   — which expresses the controlling idea
   — place it at the beginning

3 They also contain *support sentences*   — — —

   — used to develop or support the topic sentence
   — make up the bulk of the paragraph.

Plan for paragraphs   — — —

1 Start with the *topic sentence*

   — to express the controlling idea

2 Explanation or definition

   — to clarify the topic sentence
   — to remove ambiguities
   — to define abstract terms

3 a) One example in detail

        — to provide clear evidence
        — to support the controlling idea

3 b) Two or three examples in passing

        — to widen the scope

4 Conclusion

        — to show the relevance of the examples
        — to round off the paragraph
        — to draw loose ends together   — — —

Functions of paragraphs   — — —

1 Descriptive paragraphs ⎤   not usually used in the type of answer
2 Narrative paragraphs   ⎦   considered here.
3 a) Explanatory paragraphs ⎤
   b) Persuasive paragraphs ⎦— the type of paragraph to use.

Linking
Link your paragraphs together with phrases which   — — —

        — look back to what has been said previously, and
        — look ahead to what is to come next

3.1 Introduction

One can perhaps look upon paragraphs as the building blocks out of which one constructs one's answer to a question. Depending on what is required, one chooses paragraphs of different shapes and sizes just as one would choose different shapes and sizes of building materials to build a house. But this analogy gives a somewhat monolithic view of paragraphs — things without internal structure or purpose.

Perhaps a better analogy would be to regard paragraphs as the cells which go to make up a living organism. Although each cell is unique, it has functional and structural features in common with all living cells. In the same way, each paragraph, though unique, has functional and structural elements in common with other paragraphs.

In this chapter we are concerned with these two elements, so let us reflect generally for a moment on the terms 'structure' and 'function' as they relate to paragraphs. Although a paragraph itself has physical form, being made up of words set in print upon the page, the 'function' of a paragraph is an abstract concept. It means the purpose which the paragraph is supposed to fulfil. It will be shown later in the chapter that, by and large, the function of your paragraphs should be to explain or persuade.

3.2   Structure of paragraphs

In much the same way, the structure of a paragraph is an abstract concept. But this concept of structure can itself be analysed, the different parts existing on different levels of abstraction. The most abstract part of a paragraph is its 'controlling idea'; somewhat less abstract are the 'topic sentence' and the 'support sentences' which actually appear in ink on the paper. All of these features are discussed below.

It is sometimes helpful to think of the controlling idea as the soul of a paragraph, of the topic sentence as its skeleton, and of the support sentences as its flesh and blood. The appropriateness of this analogy should become apparent to you when you have studied the next three sections of this chapter.

3.2.1 The controlling idea

Each paragraph of your answer should make a single point. Put another way, each paragraph should give concrete form to a single idea. This idea unifies the paragraph: it is called the 'controlling idea.' One could say that the controlling idea summarises the paragraph. It also limits it: information not related to the controlling idea has no place in the paragraph.

Consider, for example, the answer you might make to the following question from a Politics and Government paper:

'Party discipline in the House of Commons can never be more than a process of bluff.' Is this true?

Whichever side you intend to take on this issue, you may feel it necessary to say something about the power which the party whips exercise over the minds of their members. You might therefore write as follows:

The removal of the party whip from a Member of Parliament is a powerful weapon for maintaining party discipline. Without the whip, the Member has the advantage, of course, of being free to vote on any issue as his conscience dictates. His obligation to vote with his party is removed. But so, too, is its support. As a result, his constituency committee may call him to account for his action; and it is unlikely to adopt him as its candidate in the next General Election. If he wants to stand again, it must be as an Independent, unlikely to succeed against the official candidate chosen by the party to replace him. The ever-present realisation of his probable fate will make him consider carefully the wisdom of stepping out of line and going it alone. Fear of loss of the party whip tends to make MP's, in the words of W S Gilbert, 'vote just as their leaders tell 'em to'.

The controlling idea of this paragraph is expressed in the first sentence: the effectiveness of the threat of removal of the party whip in maintaining discipline. The rest of the paragraph develops and supports this idea.

You could not in the same paragraph mention that the whip system is no more than bluff. However true you might feel this to be, it is a new idea, not contained in the controlling idea. It therefore has no place in the paragraph. If you want to discuss the question of bluff you must write a second paragraph. To discuss it in the first one will destroy that paragraph's unity.

Self-Assessment Questions
Read the following paragraph carefully. State as concisely as possible what the controlling idea seems to be. (It is not stated explicitly in the first sentence.)

Many teenagers have casual sexual relations with members of the opposite sex. They are not sure whether this is right and are sometimes worried by their uncertainty. Again, although frequently the soul of honour − with strong feelings for the under-privileged and disadvantaged − they are easily led astray by their associates. This may cause casual behaviour, lack of thought for the feelings of others, callousness, lying and even down-right stealing. They may regret their lapses from their ideals, resolving not to repeat them. But the lapses recur in spite of their good intentions.

Discussion
This paragraph seems to be about the moral behaviour of teenagers. It concerns their actions when gripped by strong conflicting forces: their ideals of what they ought to do, on the one hand; and their desires, or their need for the approval of their friends, on the other. Unlike a mature adult with the experience needed to steer safely in such troubled waters, many teenagers drift with the tide for lack of a reliable chart. They are uncertain, turbulent, unreliable; they lack confidence.

Perhaps the controlling idea of the paragraph could be expressed:

Many teenagers are morally insecure.

Self-Assessment Questions
Each of the following passages has two controlling ideas. State as concisely as possible what the two ideas are. Re-write each passage in two paragraphs, the first containing one of the controlling ideas, the second containing the other. There is no need to stick to the exact wording given.

1 The sociologist's main interest is in the relationships between people. He is likely to come from a middle-class background, and will be interested in the way relationships vary from society to society. Few sociologists are working-class because of the education system. Society could not exist without people, but the sociologist's background will influence his approach to the subject.

2 Judges are very able lawyers and tend to be somewhat remote from every-

day life: one does not meet them in a pub or a football crowd. They are more likely to be seen at a London Club or relaxing at their home in the country. They have probably achieved distinction at school and university. They need a thorough understanding of the law and must be able to see through faulty arguments from other lawyers who are also somewhat remote figures. In addition, judges must be able to marshal innumerable facts, control their courts, and protect witnesses from over-aggressive cross-questioning from counsel.

3 Handicapped children have special educational needs. Children with problems of hearing, for example, need specially trained teachers to cope with their hearing problems. There are not enough training colleges in England which specialise in audiology and the number of these needs to be increased. Blind children also need help: they need to learn Braille and other special skills to replace their lack of vision. Again, a wide range of handicapped children — maladjusted, physically disabled and so on — all need to learn special skills. And for these children there is unfortunately a shortage of specially trained teachers who have themselves learned Braille, lip-reading, sign language, physiotherapy or whatever particular children need to learn.

Discussion

1 The two main controlling ideas are:

The sociologist's main interest is in relationships between people.
His background will influence his approach.

You may have re-written the passage as follows:

The sociologist's main interest is in the relationships between people and the way these relationships vary from society to society. After all, society could not exist without people and without their forming relationships of one kind and another.
However, no sociologist can completely free himself from his own background. Because of the educational system, most sociologists tend to be middle class, very few of them coming from working-class homes. Therefore the way a sociologist approaches his subject is bound to be coloured by a certain perspective.

2 The two controlling ideas would seem to be:

Judges are very able lawyers.
They tend to be somewhat remote in their way of life.

Here is a possible way of re-organising the passage:

Judges are very able lawyers. They have probably achieved distinction at school and university. They need a thorough understanding of the law and must be able to see through faulty arguments from other lawyers. In addition, they must be able to marshal innumerable facts, control their courts, and protect witnesses from over-aggressive cross-questioning from counsel. Like other lawyers, judges tend to be somewhat remote. One seldom meets them in a pub or a football crowd. They are more likely to be seen dining at high table at an inn of court, discussing cases at a London club or relaxing at their home in the country.

3 *The two controlling ideas are:*

Handicapped children need special provision.
More training facilities are needed for specialist teachers.

Here is a possible way of splitting the paragraph into two parts to show the two different ideas:

Handicapped children have special educational needs. Children with hearing problems, for example, need to learn lip-reading and sign language. Blind children need to learn Braille and physically disabled children need to learn to develop their muscles. All such skills are essential if the children are to overcome their handicaps.
Unfortunately, there are not enough teachers to cope. More training facilities are required to train teachers in appropriate disciplines. Courses are needed which specialise in audiology, Braille, and physiotherapy and which help teachers to understand the particular frustrations experienced by all handicapped children.

3.2.2 The topic sentence

The sentence which expresses the controlling idea of a paragraph is called the 'topic sentence'. In the example quoted earlier about party discipline, the first sentence is the topic sentence:

The removal of the party whip from a Member of Parliament is a powerful weapon for maintaining party discipline.

As this sentence expresses the controlling idea – *the threat of removal of the party whip* – it is by definition the topic sentence.

The first sentence is the topic sentence also in this paragraph about Shakespeare's *Macbeth:* (The sentences are numbered in this example)

(1) Darkness seems to brood over the tragedy, many scenes taking place at night or in the menacing twilight. (2) The vision of the dagger, the murder of Duncan, the muder of Banquo, the sleep-walking of Lady Macbeth, all come in night-scenes. (3) Banquo rides homeward to meet his assassins at dusk, the hour when 'light thickens', when the wolf begins to howl and the owl to scream, and withered murder steals forth to his work. (4) Only twice does the

sun seem to shine: early on when Duncan sees the swallows flitting round Macbeth's castle; and towards the close when the English army assembles at Birnham Wood:

In this paragraph, the controlling idea is the all-pervading sense of darkness which shrouds the play. Really, one could say that it is summed up in the first seven words — 'Darkness seems to brood over the tragedy'. The first half sentence is thus, strictly speaking, the topic sentence.

The second and third sentences support the topic sentence by giving examples of events at night (Sentence 2) and in the menacing twilight (Sentence 3). Sentence 4 supports the topic sentence by providing a contrast.

The topic sentence may come at any point in the paragraph, beginning, middle or end. Indeed, a paragraph need not necessarily have a topic sentence at all; in other words, the controlling idea need not be explicitly stated. To give a somewhat trite example:

Mr Jones rose at eight o'clock, breakfasted at nine and went to the office. He had lunch at one, and tea at four thirty. He then caught his usual 5.47 train home, had supper at seven, watched television and went to bed.

The controlling idea is that *Mr Jones passed an uneventful day,* but this is not actually stated. There is thus no topic sentence. If the paragraph were re-written:

Mr Jones passed an uneventful day. He rose at eight, breakfasted at nine, etc. etc.,

the topic sentence would be the one italicised.

Until you are fairly experienced in paragraph writing, you would be well advised always to use a topic sentence, and always to place it near the beginning of the paragraph. Make it the very first sentence, in fact, unless you have a good reason for not doing so. We will mention one such reason under 'Linking Paragraphs' towards the end of this chapter. But now let us look at what the rest of the paragraph should consist of.

3.2.3 Support sentences

The rest of the paragraph should develop or support the topic sentence, by explaining it, illustrating it, exploring its possible meanings or re-stating it in somewhat different terms. The sentences which do this are called 'support sentences'. Suppose, for example, you are answering the following question from a *Certificate in Education* paper in History of Education:

To what extent did the notion of 'parity of esteem' influence the promoters of the 1944 Education Act?

Suppose that in the first paragraph, you have stated in general terms the position you will adopt in arguing your case. Suppose, also, that in your essay plan, you have allotted Paragraph Two to a definition of the phrase, 'parity of esteem'. You might write paragraph Two as follows: (Again, the sentences are numbered)

(1) What, then, did the planners of the 1944 Act mean by 'parity of esteem'? (2) They were referring to the regard which, they felt, society should pay to the three different types of secondary schools proposed under the Act. (3) The products of each type of school should be valued by society as having been educated, each according to his individual needs, in 'equal but different' schools: grammar, technical and secondary modern. (4) Children from secondary modern schools, where the emphasis would be on the development of manual skills, should be esteemed as highly as children from grammar schools in which the development of mental powers would be stressed. (5) Society should regard both types of children as being on a par with one another. (6) No longer should the label 'elementary school' mark a child as being inferior, nor should the grammar school provide the only route to a 'better' job. (7) 'Parity of esteem' was the dream of those who wanted an end to those boundaries between classes which, in their opinion, were made more rigid by the old elementary/grammar division.

In this paragraph, Sentence 1 is the 'link' with the previous paragraph (see page 38). Sentence 2 is the topic sentence. It expresses the controlling idea of the paragraph — what 'parity of esteem' meant to the people who used the phrase. Sentence 3 develops the definition by talking about children from the different schools rather than about the schools themselves. Sentence 4 develops Sentence 3 by specific example of the different human qualities to be developed in modern and grammar schools — manual or mental. Note the use of the word 'esteem' in this sentence to link it directly with the phrase 'parity of esteem' in the topic sentence. Sentence 5 is a more generalised form of Sentence 4; the phrase 'on a par' links it with 'parity' in the topic sentence.

In Sentence 6, the development follows a different line. It uses the negative form: 'No longer should the label etc.' to show what those who valued the notion of parity of esteem were attacking — that people thought the products from elementary schools inferior to those of the grammar schools. And Sentence 7 again refers to the differences between products of the different schools but in more general terms than Sentence 6. The use of the word 'dream' in Sentence 7 will allow you in the next paragraph to examine how far the notion of parity of esteem was desirable, how far it was practicable and how far it was actually achieved. Sentence 7 thus neatly rounds off the paragraph while at the same time providing a spring-board from which to jump off into paragraphs with different controlling ideas.

3.2.4 Analogies

It should now be clear why the analogy of soul, skeleton, and flesh and blood was an appropriate one to apply to the structure of paragraphs. For what gives a paragraph its life is its controlling idea — hence the use of 'soul'. And what gives that idea form is the topic sentence — hence 'skeleton'. But the paragraph needs more than just bare bones: it needs 'flesh and blood' to cover the skeleton and fill it out. Hence the need for support sentences.

Two other analogies are illuminating. One may regard the controlling idea of a paragraph as the trunk of a tree and the support sentences as its banches. Some branches stem direct from the trunk of the tree — some support sentences, in other words, stem direct from the controlling idea. Others stem from the branches. But all are part of the same tree; all grow from the same trunk; all together they develop the same controlling idea.

Another helpful analogy is to regard the paragraph as a building in which the controlling idea is the roof and the support sentences are its pillars. While all the pillars help to hold up the roof, some do so directly, others indirectly by buttressing the main support pillars. In the same way, each support sentence must support the controlling idea of the paragraph, directly or indirectly.

Try to bear in mind these analogies when writing your paragraphs. Ask yourself 'Does this sentence develop the controlling idea. Is it a branch of this tree or of another?' If of another, prune it! Alternatively, ask yourself, 'Does this sentence support the controlling idea or should it be a pillar in another building?' If the latter, demolish it, or erect it in the building where it belongs! By this means you will ensure that each paragraph develops one point well, not a host of points badly.

3.3   A plan for paragraphs

So far we have discussed support sentences as though they spring easily to your mind and flow from your pen like water from a tap! But you will very likely find that things are not so easy: even if you know your subject well, and have points to make and ideas to develop, the actual development of the paragraph is hard to achieve. Either you can think of no relevant back-up, or you write reams of not very coherent padding! In both cases, you need a definite plan for your paragraphs so that you can develop your points with maximum effectiveness.

Such a plan is the following:

1 Write your topic sentence.
2 Explain, expound or define in one or two sentences what any difficult word or phrase in the topic sentence means.
3 Give examples to back up your topic sentence.
   (a)   One should be in detail and fully explained.
   (b)   Two or three others should be mentioned in passing.
4 Round off the paragraph with a sentence which may be a modification of the topic sentence, or a clarification of exactly how the examples illustrate it.

The plan can obviously not be used for all paragraphs. Apart from anything else, your essay would be very boring if all its paragraphs were written in exactly the same order. However, suitably modified and varied, it is a useful plan for the middle of the essay where points must be made and the evidence for them adduced.

Let us consider an example of the use of the Paragraph Plan from Shakespeare's *Othello*. You are trying to show one aspect of the character of Iago, the villain of the piece, and you write as follows. (The numbers refer to the stages of the Paragraph Plan.)

1) Iago is a master of innuendo, suggestion, and insinuation. 2) In other words, he uses veiled hints, 'asides' meant to be overheard or apparent denials of unpleasant thoughts, rather than direct accusations. And he employs these indirect devices throughout his seduction of Othello. 3a) In his first attack, speaking of Cassio's hasty departure, his words

> ... I cannot think it,
> That he would steal away so guilty-like,
> Seeing you coming.

introduce the idea of a thief caught in the act, an idea which Othello had never contemplated. Iago does not say directly that Cassio is a thief: he appears to deny it. But he knows that he has in fact sown the seeds of suspicion by linking theft with Cassio in Othello's mind. 3b) Iago's next attack, his feigned reluctance to utter his thoughts because they may be 'vile and false', further arouses Othello's suspicions of Cassio. His discussion later of the infidelity shows him again spreading doubt while refraining from direct accusation. 4) Iago's use of innuendo gives a clue to his success with Othello, because jealousy by its very nature depends more on suspicion than on fact. Iago knows that Othello will be influenced more by Desdemona's possible vices than by her known virtues.

In the paragraph above, sentence 1) is the topic sentence: it gives the point you want to make about the character of Iago. However, it is one thing to use words like 'innuendo' and 'insinuation;' it is another thing to explain what you mean by them and to justify them. Hence the need for the support sentences under 2) and 3). At 2), you translate, as it were, the technical terms into simpler language – hints, asides, denials: you also use the negative form 'rather than direct accusations' to show what Iago does *not* use.

At 3a), you give one example in detail. This involves providing the context and the words of Iago – just enough of each to set the scene for your reader. You then comment on the example to show how it illustrates your point and thus supports the controlling idea of the paragraph as expressed in the topic sentence.

At 3b), you widen the scope by producing two more pieces of evidence. Remember that you are aiming to show that Iago is a 'master of innuendo', not just that he uses it on one occasion. You must therefore give as much indication as possible that he employs it frequently in his dealings with Othello. On the other hand, you have not the time to deal with each example in the same detail as you used at 3a); so you merely refer to the other examples.

At 4), you realise that you have strayed somewhat from the controlling idea of the paragraph; or at any rate that your reader may have forgotten exactly what point you were making. You therefore round off the paragraph by reference back to 'innuendo' which you mentioned in sentence 1). You also mention the reason why you feel that innuendo is an appropriate means of arousing jealousy.

There are many different ways of planning a paragraph, but the one suggested above will help to ensure that your ideas are fully developed, explained and justified. To recapitulate, the purpose of 2) — explanation and definition — is to make certain your topic sentence is fully understood and that any ambiguities in the topic sentence are cleared up. The purpose of 3a) — one example in detail — is to back up your topic sentence very closely with appropriate evidence. The purpose of 3b) is to widen the scope — to show that you can draw examples from more than just one place. And the purpose of 4) is to draw the separate strands of the paragraph together so that a clear impression of its controlling idea is left with the reader.

Self-Asssessment Question
Analyse the following paragraph by pointing out clearly:

1   the topic sentence
2   any explanation or definition
3 a) one example in detail
3 b) other examples to widen the scope
4   conclusion

Technical development seems sometimes to be more important than anything else. The latest scientific inventions, which give us more control over the physical environment, dazzle us. How incredible it is that, on a silicon chip the size of a pin-head, we can cram electronic circuitry that would have needed a small room only a few years ago! And with several of these chips put together, what brain-power can we not achieve with which to perform innumerable routine and hum-drum tasks! In the same way, look how we have harnessed the power of the atom, broken the sound barrier, extracted oil and gas from beneath the North Sea, and travelled to the moon. And these achievements seem to us more worthwhile than helping people to make sense of their lives, form stable and meaningful relationships with other people or conquer the problems of unemployment, poverty and crime which surround us. Material progress diverts our attention from such things.

Discussion

Sentence 1 states the controlling idea – that we pay more attention to technicalities than to human problems.	*Paragraph Plan (1)* *Topic sentence*
Sentence 2 expands on the phrase 'technical development, and re-states the controlling idea	*Paragraph Plan (2)* *Explanation or definition*
Sentences 3 and 4 detail one achievement – microcircuitry and the micro-processor	*Paragraph Plan (3a)* *One example in detail*
Sentence 5 mentions four other examples to widen the scope. Sentence 6 gives many examples of human problems we ignore.	*Paragraph Plan (3b)* *Many examples are mentioned*
Sentence 7 re-states the controlling idea in a different way from Sentence 1. This difference is possible because of examples previously given to illustrate the point.	*Paragraph Plan (4)* *Conclusion*

Self-Assessment Question

The following paragraph omits certain aspects described in the Paragraph Plan. Which sections are missing? Try to improve the passage by adding them at appropriate places.

The editor of a national newspaper is the impresario of a vast entertainment enterprise. His paper contains murders, political quarrels, film-stars falling in and out of love, rumours of war, men who have made millions and men who have lost them. And to include all this is the editor's proper function.

Discussion
The sections missing are:

Paragraph Plan (2):	*Some explanation of what is meant by 'the impresario of a vast entertainment enterprise'. For example: 'The editor must search far and wide to present his readers with exciting, novel or amusing items.'*
Paragraph Plan (3a):	*One example in detail*
Paragraph Plan (4):	*Some sort of conclusion*

The original author wrote the following paragraph; he omitted 3a), presumably because he wanted to concentrate on variety.

The editor of a national newspaper is the impresario of a vast entertainment enterprise. He is concerned with a ceaseless search for news that will tickle the palate at breakfast or lift the spirit on the bus journey. His paper is a three-ring circus, daily presenting to his patrons the greatest show on earth. His paper contains murders, political quarrels, film-stars falling in and out of love, rumours of war, men who have made millions, and men who have lost them. And to include all this is the editor's proper function. The journalist is traditionally an entertainer; he must entertain or find another trade.

3.4 Functions of paragraphs
Paragraphs fulfil a variety of functions:

1   Descriptive paragraphs describe an event or a scene.
2   Narrative paragraphs tell a story.
3 a) Explanatory paragraphs explain ideas.
  b) Persuasive paragraphs persuade the reader of the truth of some assertion.

In answering the kind of questions considered in this book, we are most interested in explanatory and persuasive paragraphs. We should just look briefly, however, at the descriptive and narrative kinds so as to see what to avoid. Here are two examples:

3.4.1 Descriptive paragraphs

Slaves, many brought to Rome from the provinces, worked as servants, teachers or labourers. The masters could treat their slaves how they liked; many freed them after a while if they behaved well.

Note how static the paragraph appears. It describes a situation which existed at one time. It will not help you to prove something, develop an argument, or convince someone.

If fact, if you find yourself describing things in an answer, beware! Think again! Ask yourself why the examiner needs to be told facts. Does he not probably know them already?

3.4.2 Narrative paragraph

From the beginning of 1945, Hitler hardly left the bunker under his office in Berlin. But when this was captured in May of that year no trace of him was found. He had taken poison a few days earlier and some of his followers had immediately burned his body.

Note that the paragraph does not explain or prove anything. It does not back up any argument. Event follows event without any reason being given. The paragraph simply tells a story. And this is the thing to watch. If, in an answer to a question where you should be trying to convince or persuade, you find yourself telling the story, stop! Ask yourself, why does the examiner need to be told it? Does he not know it already? And if he does, could you not refer to it as something given — some piece of data shared between you and the examiner, about which you need merely to jog his memory for him to react to it in the appropriate way?

3.4.3 Persuasive and explanatory paragraphs

In our survey of the functions of paragraphs, we have so far looked at descriptive paragraphs and at narrative paragraphs. Neither type is recommended for use where a case must be made and reasons given.

Instead one needs to use paragraphs whose function is to explain ideas or to persuade, convince, or coax the reader to accept a point of view. This function of explanation or persuasion is needed in almost every paragraph of the type of essay we are discussing.

Suppose, for instance, that you are set the question:

What is the value of trial by jury as practised in England?

You may feel that there is an overwhelming case in favour of trial by jury as against, say, trial by a panel of lay magistrates. You may feel that the majority of the legal profession support the system of trial by jury. You realise, however, that a case has been made out against it, and part of your answer must therefore set out this case as convincingly as you possibly can. One way of doing this is to set out the case almost as though it was presented by a leading proponent of the anti-jury position. For example, you might write:

Some judges argue strongly against the jury system. They express the view that a judge, sitting with a number of lay magistrates, would constitute a more experienced, knowledgeable, and hence more competent tribunal than a panel of laymen, inexperienced in criminal matters. *Judges and magistrates, after all, see many wrong-doers in the course of their work. This surely develops their nose for the criminal so that they can smell him out even when the scent is faint. Juries, on the other hand, have no such experience. They are all too easily led by the nose by a plausible rogue. And emotional appeals by learned counsel to their better feelings can sway what little judgement they possess.*

In the first two sentences, you put forward in your own voice the anti-jury position. In the next four sentences (shown italicised), by means of such phrases as *after all, surely, all to easily, and what little judgement,* you change the voice to that of one of the anti-jury judges. And in the final sentence you indicate that such a view is, at any rate, understandable.

This technique of changing voices is not of course the only method of making a convincing case. The method was chosen merely to illustrate a particular kind of paragraph. The point is that such a paragraph is neither descriptive nor narrative. Its functions are partly explanatory and partly persuasive: to explain the judges' attitude and to make this attitude convincing.

Most of your paragraphs should fulfil these latter functions.

3.5 Linking paragraphs

A good essay will lead the reader through a logical argument, making it clear to him why a particular point has been introduced and how it leads on to the next one. To write such an essay is not easy; you tend to forget that although *you* may know why you have written each particular paragraph, your reader does not He has not got your insight into the structure of the essay as a whole: he cannot look at the master-plan in your mind.

Your must therefore show him at critical places what you are planning to do, and why. The start of each paragraph is such a place because you are moving from one idea to another. Sometimes the ideas follow on naturally, but when they do not, it is as well to take trouble to link them. This may need only an appropriate word; it may need a short phrase; or it may need a whole sentence. Below are some examples:

Thus. . . .
However. . . .
But. . . .
Similarly. . . .
Nonetheless. . . .
In addition to. . . .
On the other hand. . . .
Having dealt with A, let us now turn to B . . . .
It has been shown how C . . . it is now necessary to show how D . . .
A related point is . . .
What has been said about P scarcely applies to Q . . . .
The two previous points have concerned X & Y, we must now consider Z. . . .
Whatever the cause, the effects have been widespread . . . .
A more appropriate definition might be . . . .
Not directly related to this, but still relevant is . . . .
So much for M. We must now turn to N. . . .
In clear contrast . . . .
There is some force in this argument but . . . .
Not all critics accept this view. They hold that . . . .

The possibilities are of course legion. The key to bear in mind is that a link-ing phrase must fulfil two functions: it must *look back* to what has been said, and it must *look ahead* to what is coming. Your reader will feel that he has a guide. He will not mind stopping, as it were, for a moment or two to admire the view, because you have told him that you will get him to his destination in due course.

Self-Assessment Question
Look back to pages 5, 6 and 7. Note how the paragraphs are linked together. List the link words and phrases used. Against each phrase, set down in one column.

the words which look back and in another column the words which look forward. It may help you to see how this has been done for the first two links in the discussion below. When you have looked at these two, cover the others and try yourself.

Discussion

Paragraph	Link word or phrase	Word or phrase looking back	Word or phrase looking forward
1	—	—	—
2	*These four questions...*	*'These four..'*	*(The thought continues)*
3	*Let us look a little more deeply*	*...'more'*	*'Let us look..'*
4	*But the question involves two other...*	*'But'*	*...'other..'*
5	*Secondly...*	*(implies 'first')*	*'Secondly...'*
6	*Now.... are of this sort.*	*...'of this sort'*	*('Now' implies change of the line of thought)*
7	*Which brings us...*	*'Which'...*	*'...brings us'*
8	*Let us now look...*	*(A rather abrupt change)*	*...'now'*
9	*There is first the problem...*	*(The thought continues)*	*...'first'*

Self-Assessment Question

The two paragraphs which follow show an abrupt change of subject. Link them together to give the passage as a whole a sense of continuity.

1 In his later years, Rembrandt's pictures are impressionistic. He seems to have tried, as it were, to paint light itself rather than the shapes it illuminates. The picture of Saul and David, where what attracts most attention are the jewels glistening in the head-dress, is a notable example.

2 As a young man, Rembrandt excelled at painting pictures full of realistic detail. 'The Anatomy Lesson' is an example. Here the lecturer is demonstrating a corpse to a group of doctors. The muscles of one arm have been dissected and we may be certain that the picture is anatomically correct. We see the same realism in the huge canvases depicting the various Guilds of Holland.

Discussion

Here are two ways in which Paragraph 2 might be started to give a sense of continuity with Paragraph 1:

(a) *In contrast to such impressionism, Rembrandt's earlier work is characterised by realism. He excelled at paintings full of realistic detail. . .*

(b) *Such impressionism seems a long way from the realism of his earlier years, when he excelled at paintings. . .*

(Incidentally, the historical link — arranging the paragraphs chronologically — has been purposely avoided so as to emphasise the change in style from realism to impressionism)

Assignment B

Develop *five* of the following topic sentences into well-rounded paragraphs which make your points convincingly. Treat each paragraph as a separate exercise: do not attempt to link one with another. As far as possible, use the Paragraph Plan and indicate the different stages (i.e. 1, 2, 3a, 3b, 4).

1   Our age is one of unprecedented opportunity for personal development.
2   In many ways our world discourages individual initiative.
3   Traditional moral values have become confused.
4   The authority of parents has become weakened.
5   This is an age of mass culture.
6   Semi-educated people are extremely susceptible to advertising.
7   We need people with initiative.
8   Labour-saving devices can be a blessing.
9   Labour-saving devices are not a recipe for happiness.
10 Our civilisation is a very materialistic one.
11 Democracy works by persuasion.
12 Nowadays, no important problem is a self-contained, local problem.
13 Some people think that communication consists primarily of exposition.
14 The basis of communication is shared feeling.
15 The great defect of our education system is the need for too early specialisation.

Send your Assignment to your tutor. Before you do so, check to see that in each paragraph you have followed the Paragraph Plan of Section 3.3 (page 32)

4.Order:The jury approach

Summary
In this unit the following points are covered. (Students are recommended
to fill in the page numbers as an aid to revision)   *Page*

Your answer needs three clearly defined sections: beginning, middle
and end.   — — —

The beginning
Clarify the question and analyse the issues.   — — —

The Middle   — — —
Avoid the following faults:
1 the chronological approach   — — —
2 the vascillating approach   — — —
3 the 'damp squib.'   — — —

Present the evidence on both sides.
Group your paragraphs according to appropriate criteria.   — — —

The End   — — —
Your conclusion should take the form of a verdict. Say where
you consider the truth of the matter to lie. It is perfectly legitimate to remain neutral: to return a non-proven verdict.
Avoid the phrase 'Thus we see. . .' in your last paragraph.   — — —

4.1   Introduction

The order in which you set out your points is of considerable importance in
any analytical essay. As Aristotle said about tragedies, they cannot just start or
stop at any point: they must have a clearly defined beginning, middle and end.
   This unit and the next consider two ways of arranging your answer to an
examination question in a logical order. In this unit, we are concerned with the
'jury' approach, so called, because your verdict or judgement is made at the end
of the essay in the same way that the jury in a court case delivers its verdict after
listening to the evidence from both sides. As in court, therefore, you build up to
your conclusion gradually, establishing one important point after another.

4.2   The beginning

The beginning of your answer prepares the examiner for what is to come. It

43

must make an impact upon him. Do not take too long in getting to the point. Do not beat about the bush. Start straight in — *in medias res,* (in the middle of things) as Horace wrote about poetry.

With the jury approach, you begin by clarifying the question and analysing the issues to be discussed. How to do this has been described in Unit 2. Suppose for example, you are answering the following question:

'Television is the opium of the people.' To what extent does this modern version of Marx's dictum sum up the attitude of people today?

Here is a possible way of beginning your answer:

Marx's remark, that religion was the opium of the people, was directed against the Church. He meant that organised religion directed the attention of the masses away from the misery of the present world towards the expected joys of the world to come. The much advertised solaces of religion numbed the senses of the poor and oppressed just as effectively as opium. The modern version differs from Marx in that television replaces religion as the pain-killer. Another difference is in the nature of the misery. For whereas physical suffering and hardship was a common experience in Marx's time, the problem today is more psychological. Alienation, that helplessness of the individual in the face of the impersonal forces of the state, overwhelms the majority of us. We turn therefore to television for relief and escape. And in doing so, we become the slaves of the television promoters. Or so at least the statement would have us think.

So far your remarks have been perfectly general. You certainly have not committed yourself to an opinion one way or the other: it is still open to you to agree with the statement or to disagree with it as you choose. You have, however, clarified the issue. You have made it clear that the statement means that television is something which takes our minds off our troubles and lures us into a torpor, leaving us incapable of positive action to improve our situation.

4.3 The middle
You have completed your opening remarks and are ready to deal with specific points. You have arrived therefore at the middle section of the essay. Here we are concerned with the main bulk of the evidence you present to the examiner. In what order should you arrange it?

There are some obvious faults of arrangement which you should try to avoid. Let us take a look at three of these.

4.3.1 Fault 1: The chronological approach
Avoid any sort of time sequence. Don't tell the *story,* in an English Literature question; don't give the *history* of the Second World War as an answer to a question on British Foreign Policy; don't give a chronological account of the

development of, say, nineteenth century Germany in a question on the rise of nationalism. If you do so, you will almost certainly *not* be answering the question. You will not be proving points; you will be merely stating facts, and tracing the progress of events.

4.3.2 Fault 2: The vascillating approach
Avoid shifting continually from side to side in your argument. To do so tends to confuse the reader, who is left wondering which side you are supporting. Suppose for example you are answering the question:

'Professional associations are trade unions for gentlemen.' Discuss.

You will merely muddle your reader if you order your paragraphs in the following manner:

1 Like trade unions, professional associations act as pressure groups to improve the pay of their members.
2 But they do not appear to go on strike so often.
3 They arrange social facilities for their members.
4 But these tend to be more sophisticated than those of trade unions.
5 However, like unions, professional associations negotiate conditions of employment of their members.
6 But these conditions frequently concern how their members should relate to the public rather than to their employers.
7 On the other hand professional associations operate restrictive practices, like some unions.
8 However, the professional associations justify these practices in terms of service to the public, not self-interest.

The argument of such an essay seems to go up and down like a yo-yo! Or, like evenly matched armies, first one side seems to be winning, then the other. It would probably be clearer for the reader if you set out together all the points in favour of the case, and then dealt with all the points against it. We will look closer at this method later, but there is one more obvious fault to avoid, which we must look at first.

4.3.3 Fault 3: The damp squib
Avoid starting strongly and then petering out: don't fire all your big guns in the first few paragraphs. You will have no ammunition left at the end. Your final paragraphs will seem somewhat lame and you will have to finish – in the words of T S Eliot – 'Not with a bang but a whimper'.

4.3.4 How these faults can be avoided
These three faults should if possible be avoided. Let us look now at how the Jury Approach helps you to do so. You need to present your evidence on both

sides. Suppose that in answering the Television question mentioned earlier you have jotted down the following points:

- Television shows you only what its producers want you to see.
- The selection is not your own, but someone else's.
- TV opens a world of experiences to you which you could not otherwise see or hear about.
- Watching television, you do not participate socially as you would do in the crowd at a match or in the audience at the theatre.
- TV standards are so high that it is hard for local amateur groups to compete: local talent does not therefore develop.
- TV allows you to experience the very best music and drama available.
- It enables you to see politicians and 'rulers', not just to read about them.
- TV viewers sit passively absorbing what is offered to them, like sponges soaking up water.
- Television stars are valued, not for their intrinsic worth, but for their ability to shine on TV.

How are you to arrange these points?

Not as they are, certainly! They are set out higgledy-piggledly, points supporting the value of television interspersed with points attacking it. This arrangement will muddle the reader.

Before you continue reading, try to arrange the points in a logical order.

It is almost always best to deal first with all points on one side of an argument and then to deal with points on the other. If you adopt this advice you might group your points as follows:

1 Television stars are not valued for their intrinsic worth but for their ability to shine on TV.
2 TV standards are so high that it is hard for local groups to compete: local talent does not therefore develop.
3 Watching television, you do not participate socially as you would do in a crowd at a match, or in the audience at the theatre.
4 TV viewers sit passively, absorbing what is offered to them, like sponges soaking up water.
5 TV shows you only what its producers want you to see.
6 The selection is not your own, but someone else's.
7 TV opens a world of experiences to you which you could not otherwise see or hear about.
8 It enables you to experience the very best music and drama available.
9 It enables you to see politicians and 'rulers', not just to read about them.

Here, the first six points attack the value of TV and the last three points show its good points. Thus there are two distinct groups of points — those *for* and *those against.*

In addition, the first six points are grouped in pairs: points 1) and 2) deal with what might be called the television personality cult; points 3) and 4) are concerned with audience behaviour; points 5) and 6) are concerned with the highly selective nature of TV.

In a similar manner, points 7), 8) and 9) form a group, all showing the value of TV in widening your experience. Points 8) and 9) are perhaps best regarded as special cases of point 7), but they are important enough to warrant paragraphs to themselves.

The criteria you use to relate your points with one another will differ in different cases; here you have chosen *personality cult, audience behaviour, selectiveness* and *the experiences made available by television.* You must decide which criteria will best suit your particular answer and group your points accordingly.

Self-Assessment Question

Suppose you are writing an answer to the question

Are there any circumstances in which capital punishment for murder is justified?

Suppose, too, that in your view there are a few cases when you would support the death penalty, but that by and large you are against it. And you have listed the following points you wish to make:

1   Many murderers have never had a chance. They are ill, not wicked.
2   If motives and other 'subjective' criteria are taken into account when deciding whether or not a murderer should hang, where is the dividing line between capital and non-capital crimes to be drawn?
3   Although all murders have the same outcome − a corpse − it is not possible to generalise on the treatment of the murderers, each of whom has his/her own specific motive.
4   Capital punishment for murder with a political motive may make things worse by turning the murderer into a martyr.
5   To execute someone is to admit that society has failed to educate him to keep its laws.
6   No-one has the right to deprive a fellow human being of his life.
7   Capital punishment should be re-introduced for someone who murders a police officer.
8   It is hardly ever possible to be absolutely certain that the accused is guilty.
9   On the whole, there is a stronger case for allowing capital punishment in certain circumstances than for barring it altogether.
10 Once a man has been hanged it does not help him if he is later found to be innocent.

11   To some extent one must judge what is right by the climate of the times.
12   There is sadistic satisfaction gained from knowing that a murderer is to be executed, and this corrupts society.
13   The case against capital punishment is a strong one.
14   There is a forceful argument in favour of executing those who kill while committing armed robbery.

a) Arrange these points in the most appropriate order, using the Jury Approach.
b) What criteria have you followed in deciding your chosen order?

Discussion
a) There are several ways of arranging your answer, but here is a possible order.

- *Although all murders have the same outcome – a corpse – one cannot generalise on the treatment of the murderers, each of whom has his/her own specific motive. (3)*
- *But if motives and other 'subjective' criteria are taken into account when deciding whether or not a murderer should hang, where is the dividing line between capital and non-capital crimes to be drawn? (2)*
- *Quite apart from the problem of drawing lines, the case against capital punishment is a strong one. (13)*
- *It is hardly ever possible to be absolutely certain that the accused is guilty. (8)*
- *Once a man has been hanged, it does not help him if he is later found to be innocent. (10)*
- *To execute someone is to admit that society has failed to educate him to keep its laws. (5)*
- *Many murderers have never had a chance; they are ill not wicked. (1)*
- *There is a sadistic satisfaction gained from knowing that a murderer is to be executed, and this corrupts society. (12)*
- *No-one has the right to deprive a fellow human-being of his life. (6)*
- *There is a forceful argument in favour of executing those who kill while committing armed robbery. (14)*
- *Capital punishment should be reintroduced for someone who murders a police officer. (7)*
- *Capital punishment for murder with a political motive may make things worse by turning the murderer into a martyr. (4)*
- *To some extent one must judge what is right by the climate of the times (11)*
- *On the whole, there is a stronger case for allowing capital punishment in certain circumstances than for barring it altogether. (9)*

The criteria which have been used in arriving at this order of paragraphs are discussed below:

Opening   *In line with the Jury Approach, basic issues of capital punishment are discussed in the opening paragraphs. We are trying to*

	show that we are dealing with a complex question, with points to be made both for and against capital punishment.
Middle Section	*We develop arguments against capital punishment, starting with practical problems of the uncertainty of guilt; leading on to problems about society; and finally dealing with the strongest argument against capital punishment – the absolute principle, 'Thou shalt not kill.'*
	We then mention circumstances in which we feel that capital punishment is justified – armed robbery and killing policemen.
	We use the example of a political murder to illustrate that however 'right' we may feel it to be to execute a political killer, to do so may be counter-productive – his cause might prosper after his death (Remember John Brown's body!)
Conclusion*	*The example just given leads us on to consider whether we can say dogmatically that capital punishment should never be employed. The climate of the times may change. We conclude that it is best to keep our options open – ie. reserve capital punishment for the circumstances mentioned.*

4.4 The end

It is probably harder to end an examination answer convincingly than it is to start it or to write the middle. The beginning is easy! You analyse the question. The middle, too, is not all that hard. You make your points one by one and present your evidence for each.

But when you have done that, what is left? You have probably used up all your material! But your ending will be too abrupt if you just stop writing after your last point. If it is a minor point, your essay will tend to fizzle out. If it is a strong one, you will leave your reader with the impression that it is the only one which really matters, or at any rate, he may feel that you have over-emphasised the point. Some sort of rounding off is needed.

By way of analogy, compare your essay with a detective story. The arrest of the murderer is hardly ever the end, even though it is probably the climax. The detective usually gets the last word. He may tell you what first put him on the scent, or what finally convinced him that his hunch was correct.

So it is with examination questions. They need a conclusion.

In the Jury Approach, your conclusion will take the form of a verdict. You need to say, having discussed the issues thoroughly and presented the evidence, where you consider the truth of the matter to lie. In legal terms, you must 'consider your verdict'.

---

*The next section deals in more detail with how to end your answer.

Five possibilities are dealt with in the next unit. There you will be advised to make your mind up on one side or the other (for or against) if you adopt the Advocate Approach. To do so is not however necessary if you adopt the jury method where it is perfectly legitimate to remain neutral – to return a 'not proven' verdict. If you really feel that the issue cannot be decided one way or the other, you are entitled to say so.

If you decided to remain neutral in the question we have been considering, your final paragraphs might run:

Whether television acts as an 'opiate' or not depends on one's view of the people it is supposed to influence. If one thinks that the majority of one's fellow men are by and large demoralised, have fallen a victim to the manipulators of the mass media, and are unwilling to exert themselves actively to improve their lot, one might agree with the statement: television is indeed the opium of the people. If on the other hand one sees mankind as struggling to do better, watching television for recreative enjoyment, one will probably reject the statement: television is a source of real pleasure and a stimulus.

However, it seems impossible to generalise about mankind in either of these two ways; people vary such a lot. It is thus probably wisest to return an open verdict: like all inventions, television is morally neutral, neither good nor bad. What matters is how people decide to use it, and this will depend upon them, not upon television.

Here you have, as it were, sat on the fence. You have not committed yourself one way or the other. Had you done so, you would have had to write a very different ending.

4.4.1 'Thus we see'...

Finally, a word of caution. Avoid the phrase, 'Thus we see' . . . when writing your conclusion. For example, if you are answering the question,

'The New Men is dominated by a general struggle for power.' Do you agree?

avoid writing as your final sentence,

'Thus we see that The New Men is dominated by a general struggle for power.

On the face of it, this ending appears neat. You have used all your evidence and have reached the conclusion that the original statement was correct. But wait a minute! Is it really as simple as that? After all your weighty points, can you really go back to the place from which you started? Has nothing changed? It seems unlikely.

This type of conclusion is not really very strong. It is not for nothing that an Examining Board has recently complained strongly about 'lame two line conclusions, often preceded by the bane of examiners' lives: "Thus we see that"...'

The point is that the phrase gives a spurious logic to the answer. Occasionally, perhaps, it is justified: the conclusion really does follow from the body of the essay. All too often, however, the conclusion does not follow logically at all. It appears 'yoked by violence' to the rest of the essay, as Dr Johnson described the linking of ideas in metaphysical poetry.

Assignment C

Using the Jury Approach, answer the question discussed earlier:

Are there any circumstances in which capital punishment for murder is justified?

Use as many of the ideas quoted as you like. You may even use the plan exactly as it has been set out. Alternatively, you can take the opposite side — in other words, say that there are no circumstances in which capital punishment is justified — but in this case you must deal with arguments in favour of it. That is, you must yourself present your opponent's objections and demolish his likely arguments.

The purpose of this Assignment is fourfold:

1 for you to practise *developing* paragraphs again,
2 for you to practise *linking* paragraphs, and
3 for you to practise setting out your paragraphs in a *logical order*.
4 for you to gain experience of the Jury Approach.

Limit your answer to 1000 words. Remember, quality counts for more than quantity. Once you have started writing the actual answer, do not allow yourself more than 2 hours. Time yourself, and let your tutor have a note of the exact time taken.

5. Order: The advocate approach

> What we call the beginning is often the end
> And to make an end is to make a beginning.
> The end is where we start from.
>
> T S Eliot

Summary
The following points are covered: (Insert page numbers as an aid
to revision)   *Page*

The beginning:
(a) Get straight to the point   — — —
(b) There are Five Possible Verdicts: — — —
     One: The statement is *completely true.*
     Two: There is *a considerable measure of truth* in it
     Three:. The arguments for and against are *evenly balanced*
     Four   There is *not much truth* in the statement
     Five: There is *no truth* in it
(c) Adopt either Verdict Two or Verdict Four   — — —
(d) Analyse the question thoroughly   — — —

The Middle
(a) Present your evidence point by point   — — —
(b) The Three-Phase Order Plan   — — —
     Phase one: Dispose of all those points which might   — — —
                  appear to contradict your general line of
                  argument
     Phase Two: Make the points which support your case.   — — —
     Phase Three: Deal with minor points first and work up to more
                  important ones.   — — —

The end
Place the subject in its context   — — —

Jury and Advocate Approaches compared
The Jury Approach is the *safer*
The Advocate Approach is the *stronger,* but has two dangers: — — —
1 The danger of 'the unreasoned diatribe'.
2 The danger of changing sides in mid-essay.

5.1   Introduction

We now consider the 'advocate method' of writing an answer. Here you are, in
effect, pleading your case in front of a judge, the examiner.

5.2 The beginning

The key to the advocate method is to get straight to the point: answer the question straightaway. For example, a BSc (Economics) paper on English Constitutional History asked candidates to discuss the assertion that

"Pitt the Younger was pre-eminently an eighteenth century politican."

A straight answer would be:

There is a large measure of truth in this assertion.

The candidate's view has been made clear right from the start. This makes for a strong opening. The reader is left in no doubt what line the writer will take.

Again, an MA paper in Education asked candidates to 'discuss the effectiveness of the University Grants Committee as a planning body.' A direct answer would be:

As a planning body, the University Grants Committee is not particularly effective.

Again the examiner is left in no doubt as to the candidate's main drift.*

Though both answers suggested above require considerable justification, both get straight to the point. The examiner knows the line you are going to take in your answer; he can weigh your arguments and the evidence you use to support your case as he reads.

If, for example, you continue your answer on the University Grants Committee with a paragraph about the usefulness of the U.G.C. in allotting financial resources among universities, the examiner is fairly safe to assume that you are doing this only to say at a later stage that resource allocation, though a useful ancillary function, is not a major planning function. He knows that the weight of your argument will be *against* the U.G.C. as a planning body. You have already told him so. He is able to slot your remarks about allotting financial resources into an overall framework; he has some inkling of why you are making the point and this helps him to assess its contribution to your answer as he goes along.

5.2.1 The five possible verdicts

Accepting therefore that in the advocate method you must get straight to the point, let us consider what possible answers you can give to the questions asked.

---

*A much more concrete example is illuminating. You want to get to Bond Street. You stop someone in the street and ask him the way. He treats you to a dissertation on the history of London Transport, and on the relative merits of tube or bus. You would surely prefer him to tell you to 'take any bus from this stop and get off at Green Park.' If he then discussed relative merits of different modes of transport, you would place them in the context of his initial instructions. Or you could thank him and jump on the bus!

Now, it may appear to be a gross oversimplification, but when you come to think about it, you will see that there are really only *five* possible ways of giving a judgement. You are being asked in effect, 'to what extent is a certain statement true?' and you have a choice of only five possible verdicts. They are as follows:

Verdict One: The statement is *completely true.*
Verdict Two: There is *a considerable measure of truth* in it.
Verdict Three: The arguments for and against are *evenly balanced.*
Verdict Four: There is *not much truth* in the statement.
Verdict Five: There is *no truth* in it.

5.2.2 Verdicts One and Five

Let us start by considering Verdicts One and Five which express either complete agreement or complete disagreement with a given statement. You would be wise to choose neither. Why? For two reasons. First, questions involving abstract terms are imprecise. There is always room for a modicum of doubt about the terms; it is therefore rash to be dogmatic in giving an answer. The second reason is a more pragmatic one. However the question may be phrased, the examiner's aim is to assess your skill in weighing up arguments for and against a position. He therefore chooses contentious questions in which there are points to be made on both sides. Steer clear, therefore, of answers which allow no points at all to one side. Steer clear of Verdicts One and Five.

To illustrate the danger of complete agreement or disagreement, let us look at a question from an A-level History paper.

'The time has come to re-assess the character of George III.' Do you agree?

An opening according to the Verdict One formula might run:

I quite agree. George III's character has been wrongly assessed by every biographer and historian who has written about him, because none of them had access to recent medical discoveries concerning insanity. These discoveries are directly relevant to George III, etc., etc.

One does not need to be a historian to guess that this line of argument is likely to fall on stony ground as far as an examiner is concerned. Surely *some* aspects of George III's character have been properly assessed, at least during certain periods of his life. Complete agreement with a given statement is almost certain to be unsupportable with evidence.

Then what about Verdict Five — complete disagreement? A verdict Five reply to the George III question might start with the assertion that there was no need at all to re-assess the King's character. The definitive biography had been written, and no new facts or theories concerning his life or his times could possibly change the assessment already made.

This, too, is unlikely. Historians are continually reinterpreting events in the light of their greater understanding of earlier times. Besides this, our understanding of 'character' is also changing as psychologists delve more and more into the hidden depths of man's make-up and analyse actions in terms of hitherto unrealised motives.

The point is that by choosing either complete agreement or complete disagreement, you will have to defend an extreme position. Even a small amount of evidence in favour of the opposite side to the one taken will destroy your absolute stance. And examiners being what they are, they will all the time be looking for loopholes in your argument. 'Aha,' they will say. 'He's overlooked recent research by H. I. Storian which modifies the position somewhat.' And out will come the red pencil!

In a nutshell, then, it is wise to avoid Verdicts One and Five. Avoid complete agreement and complete disagreement.

5.2.3 Verdict Three

Let us turn then to the kind of answer in which the candidate comes to no conclusion: what one might call 'the fence-sitter's answer'. By and large, it is not recommended. For one thing, it is unlikely that arguments can be exactly balanced, or at any rate that the candidate has no preference for one side or the other. For another, it is a somewhat cowardly approach: it dodges the issue. One would take a rather dim view of a court of law which could not arrive at a verdict. And as a candidate you are being given a task similar to that of a court: You are being told 'Weigh the evidence and deliver your verdict'. Even if you choose the advocate's approach, which is to state your position at the outset, you will not be doing what you are asked to do unless you give a decision on one side or another.

For these reasons, Verdict Three is not recommended. You should come down off the fence. Or, to change the metaphor, you should let the balance tip one way or the other.

5.2.4 Verdicts Two and Four

By process of elimination, the way to answer is either to accept the statement with certain reservations, or to reject the statement while conceding a measure of truth to it. In other words, you should have the courage of your convictions, and take 'a line'.

By and large, if you know your subject matter throroughly, you will react instantly one way or the other to a question. Other things being equal you should trust your first reactions, and set about marshalling the evidence in favour of your 'line' while looking carefully at the same time for arguments against it. It should then follow, other things being equal, that after a few minutes' reflection, you see your way to supporting your position, and you can start to write your answer. First impressions are often best!

It may be, however, that when you start to assemble your points for and against, you find that your initial 'hunch' was wrong. In that case, you must of course change your verdict from Verdict Two to Verdict Four, or *vice versa*.

To sum up: in the 'advocate' style of answer, the first paragraph should indicate the general trend of your answer, which will almost certainly be either Verdict Two or Verdict Four. The paragraph may even indicate the kinds of arguments you will be considering. The reader will then know what to expect. And this is helpful to him in passing judgement on what he reads next. For his mind is not just a blank! He is likely to be wondering 'Why am I being told these particular views? How are they relevant to the question asked?' This propensity of a reader to reflect on the writer's motives is particularly true of the examiner, who knows the subject well. A question has been asked and he wants to know *why* the candidate is doing what he is doing — quoting examples, perhaps, or setting out the background. Too much beating about the bush makes an examiner ask himself 'When will the candidate get to the point?'

5.2.5 Analysis of the question

Having indicated in your first paragraph the line you are going to take in your answer, you should in your next paragraph or two analyse the question. How to do this has been discussed in some detail in Unit II. It may be worth your while to glance back to that unit to refresh your memory, bearing in mind particularly that a thorough analysis of the question is the foundation upon which you will build your answer.

Self-Assessment Questions

'Deliver your verdict' (in one or two sentences only) on the following questions. You may know very little about some of them, but do not let this deter you from giving a verdict. In each case, indicate words that will probably need definition in an analysis paragraph.

1 To what extent do you agree that each man's language bears the stamp of his personality?
2 'The use of prefects in school serves only to strengthen the hand of authority at the expense of the pupils.' Discuss.
3 'Latin is a language as dead as dead can be.' Is it?
4 'Disease can never be eliminated from human society.' Discuss.

Discussion

Each of the examples given probably requires a Verdict Two or Verdict Four answer. Here are some possibilities:

1 To a considerable extent it would seem true to say that each man's language bears the stamp of his personality. In order to justify this assertion, however, we must look in some detail at variations in language between individuals and at how we are employing the over-worked term 'personality'.

2 *There is really not much truth in this assertion. Prefects serve many useful functions which benefit their fellow students directly. It must however be conceded that, etc.*

3 *If by 'dead' is meant that the language is not used anywhere today as the mother tongue of children, then the old schoolboys' rhyme is undoubtedly true. What is more interesting, however, is the sense in which Latin – by language and culture–has influenced our lives in one way and another,and in this sense Latin is to some extent still alive.*

4 *Though many former illnesses are virtually unknown today, thanks to modern drugs, the somewhat pessimistic statement about disease in society is probably a fair assessment of the overall position.*

5.3 The middle

You are now in a position to present evidence to support your view. You must also mention points which do not support it – or even weaken it.

In what order should you arrange your evidence? You will of course avoid the faults mentioned earlier – the chronological approach, the vascillating approach and the damp squib. You would be well advised, too, to use some clear plan to prevent your reader's attention from flagging. Although many plans are possible, here is one which should serve you well.

5.3.1 Three-Phase Order Plan
PHASE ONE

Dispose of all those points which might appear to contradict your general line of argument.

Suppose for example, that you are answering the following question in an Economic Geography paper:

To what extent do geographical factors influence the use for transport of the Mississippi river system?

The key to this question is the word 'geographical'. If you define this in such a way as to *exclude* the economic, demographic and cultural aspects of the river system, you will probably deliver a Verdict Four judgement:

Geographical factors influence the use for transport of the Mississippi river system *to only a limited extent.*

Let us suppose that you have decided to adopt this line of approach and that you have defined what you mean by 'geographical', mentioning that you include only the physical and climatic features of the region.

You are ready, adopting Phase One of the Order Plan, to *dispose of all those points which might appear to contradict your general line of argument.* You therefore show how physical and climatic factors influence the use of the Mississippi, allotting a paragraph to each. Here is where you use your detailed knowledge of the subject: the effect of mud brought in by the Missouri, the very gentle slope of the valley, the huge winding curves, the effects of heavy rain and melting of snow, and the influence of those phenomena on the types of barges and passenger steamers used.

PHASE TWO

Make the points which support your case.

You have dealt with the contrary arguments. You now demonstrate the strength of your own case.

In continuing, therefore, to answer the Mississippi transport question you show the influence of the economic, demographic and cultural factors on the use of the river system, again allotting a paragraph to each factor. You will have a lot to write here because your contention is that these non-geographical factors outweigh the geographical ones. You will possibly mention the major centres of population, the types of trade, the recent flood control measures and changes brought about by technology.

By dealing with the points in this order, you will leave your reader with the impression that what you have defined as the geographical factors have a more limited influence than the other factors: you have devoted more space to non-geographical factors and have left them to the last. But you will have dealt fairly with the points which do not support your case. The examiner will not therefore be able to criticise you for omitting inconvenient evidence which might be used against you. Provided your definition of what you consider geographical, and what not, is reasonable and that you produce evidence to support your views, the examiner should be more than satisfied.

Phases One and Two of the Order Plan — grouping together first those points against your case and second those in favour of it — will help you to avoid the 'chronological' and 'vascillating' faults mentioned in Unit 4. Phase Three of the Plan should help you to avoid the fault of 'petering out'. The problem is how to deal with minor points so that they do not seem mere afterthoughts.

PHASE THREE

Deal with minor points first, and work up to more important ones.

There are certain snags in following Phase Three. In an examination, you must devote most of your time to major points; to deal with minor ones first may distract you from your main aim.

In addition, the advice to build up from weak to strong is the exact opposite to what was recommended in the Plan for Paragraphs in Unit 3. There it was suggested that, in supporting your topic sentence, you should give first an example in detail and then refer to two or three other examples in passing.

These two snags high-light a general point. There is no one 'correct' answer to the type of question we are considering, and there is no one 'perfect' order for dealing with points. You are, of course, free to vary the order as you see fit: variety is the spice of life. Nevertheless, you should think carefully about order, bearing in mind the faults which the Three-Phase Plan is designed to put right.

Self Assessment Question
You are taking the position that the American Democratic party should be supported rather than the Republican. You have four points to make in favour of the Democrats:

1 They have the better policy to achieve racial harmony.
2 Their symbol of the donkey is attractive.
3 They have always been the party of social reform.
4 Their leader is Mr Carter.

Remembering the Three-phase Order plan, arrange these points in an appropriate order.

Discussion
Here are the points arranged in ascending order of importance:

1 The Democrats' symbol is attractive.
2 Their leader is Mr Carter.
3 They have the better policy to achieve racial harmony.
4 They have always been the party of social reform.

Your priorities may not be exactly the same as these, but you probably agree that the donkey symbol is the least important. If you felt that you should include a point about people you know being Democrat, you would probably give that a low priority too!

5.4   The end
How should you wind up your answer if you have announced your verdict at the beginning? In a short essay — all you have time for in an examination — you cannot repeat the verdict. This would be tedious and unnecessary.

Perhaps the most satisfactory ending is one where you place the subject in a wider context. Suppose, for instance, you are answering the question 'To what extent were Henry VII and Henry VIII successful in controlling Ireland.' You have taken the line that they were not particularly successful, and you have backed up this line of argument with examples of their few successes and their many set-backs. You have run out of arguments and you have run out of time! What are you to do?

Place the subject in its context.

Your might choose a *historical context*. For example:

England had experienced difficulties in Ireland for many years before the Henrys became involved. And during the reigns of their successors, troubles continued to brew. Only in the last years of Elizabeth did Ireland at last, though temporarily, succumb to English arms.

Here you have taken a historical perspective. Having looked in detail in the body of your essay at the reigns of Henry VII and VIII, you set that short period of history against the background of a much longer time scale.

Alternatively, you might choose a wider *political context*. For example:

Ireland was only one of many issues with which the Tudors had to grapple during their reigns. Henry VII sought to re-establish the power of the monarchy over the temporal lords. Henry VIII, by dissolving the monasteries, gained power over the lords ecclesiastical. Both pursued, in other words, a centralist authoritarian policy. Their attempts to control Ireland are in line with this policy: significant, because they concern a part of the kingdom; but not perhaps as important as uniting England, as establishing better relations with France, or as gaining control of the Church.

Here you have looked at the political scene. You have compared the problem of Ireland with some of the other problems which the Tudors faced.

Which wider context you choose will depend on the particular question and on your attitude towards it. Try always to place the subject against the background which is most appropriate for it. An answer about the pros and cons of local government might be placed against a national government background; an answer about *Hamlet* might be set against Shakespeare's tragedies in general; a question on strike action could usefully be looked at against the background of industrial conflict in general.

What is important is that you try to look beyond the narrow confines of the question to wider issues — that you move from the specific to the more general.

To see why this is valuable, consider the thought behind the questions set by (usually) a panel of examiners. Their job is to select from a wide range a small topic for you to fasten your attention upon. The examiner who is faced with your particular answer will wish to see that you are capable of arguing urgently from both sides of the question. He also wants to find out how much you have understood the *significance* of the issues. Remember, too, that things are significant, not merely in themselves, but in their relation to other issues. These, then, are the reasons for the importance of looking at the question in breadth as well as depth. It puts the subject in perspective.

Self-Assessment Questions
Suggest a context in which to place each of the following subjects so as to form a concluding paragraph:

1 'Censorship of films has no place in England today.' Discuss.
2 'The Trades Unions are holding the country to ransome.' Do you agree?
3 'The Women's Liberation movement is long overdue.' Is it?

Discussion
You may have chosen some of the following contexts:

1 Censorship
- *historical: perhaps censorship was important during the early days of cinema.*
- *geographical: censorship differs in different parts of the world (compare totalitarian with democratic countries).*
- *comparison with other media: censorship of books, plays, art.*

2 Trades Unions:
- *geographical: comparison with other countries*
- *historical: present activities in comparison with the past achievements of Trades Unions.*
- *wage bargaining activities as only one aspect of the function of Trades Union; but an important aspect.*

3 Women's Liberation
- *geographical: comparison with other countries*
- *comparison with other movements: black power, prison reform, factory conditions, mental health, freedom from hunger in the Third World, etc.*
- *historical: is Women's Lib. merely an extension of the Suffragette movement of the early twentieth century?*

5.5 Impact of your answer on the reader
Not all your paragraphs will strike the reader with the same force. Your major and minor points will make different impacts upon him. So, too will your beginning and ending.

The diagram opposite gives a crude representation of the sort of variation you will achieve if you follow the Advocate Approach outlined in this unit. For the purpose of illustration, an eleven-paragraph answer has been assumed, three paragraphs comprising the beginning, seven the middle, and one the end. The height to which the paragraph blocks rise is a measure of the impact on the reader.

It can be seen that the essay starts fairly strongly: that the points *against* the argument build up from weak to medium strength; that the points *for* the argument build up from weak to strong; and that the essay concludes in a moderately strong vein.

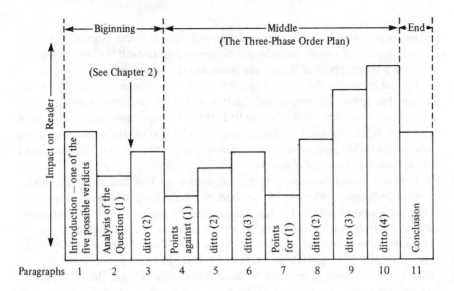

The diagram labels (left to right):

Beginning — Middle (The Three-Phase Order Plan) — End

(See Chapter 2)

Impact on Reader →

- Introduction — one of the five possible verdicts
- Analysis of the Question (1)
- ditto (2)
- Points against (1)
- ditto (2)
- ditto (3)
- Points for (1)
- ditto (2)
- ditto (3)
- ditto (4)
- Conclusion

Paragraphs 1 2 3 4 5 6 7 8 9 10 11

5.6 Jury and advocate approaches compared

The Jury Approach is the safer of the two, particularly for beginners. It is all too easy, if you feel strongly about a subject, to launch out into some unreasoned diatribe in favour of your own view without considering at all any weaknesses in your argument. This is especially the danger in such subjects as modern history, politics and sociology where you may have a strong emotional commitment to one side or the other. If you have to wait to the end to express your opinion, your answer is less likely to be tainted with bias. You will have had to analyse the subject and to present evidence on both sides first.

If you use the Jury Approach you will also avoid the danger of starting to write in support of one side, only to realise half-way through your answer that the bulk of your evidence supports the other.

It is this possibility — that your conclusion may have to be changed in the light of your evidence — which is another reason why many teachers say that your opinion should come at the end. They like the sequence — first analysis, then evidence, and finally opinion.

Supporters of the Advocate Approach, however, would argue that there is something rather naive in the view that you will not know your conclusion until you have written out the arguments on both sides. They would say that in this respect an answer involving judgement is quite unlike a solution to a mathematical problem, for example: there you must go through a mathematical process, showing your working at each stage before arriving at the answer. To give a judgement is also unlike telling a story, where the author usually proceeds in chronological order.

The point such teachers would make is fairly straightforward. If you are asked to give a judgement, you might as well state it at the beginning of your answer, having of course thought out before you do so both the evidence which you will use in support of it, and any reservations you may have.

By and large, the Advocate Approach would seem the more forceful, in that its aim throughout is constant and clearly stated: to persuade the reader of a particular point of view. Skilfully handled, the Advocate Approach should serve you well. It has the great advantage that it forces you to take a position on one side or the other and to defend it against any possible attack. 'This is what I think,' you say, 'and this is why I think it.'

But you should beware of being too dogmatic. You are, after all, making a *value* judgement. Whether in the field of ethics, aesthetics, politics or whatever, your answer cannot be conclusive. Someone else, with different attitudes and a different background, has a perfect right to take the opposite line to yours. It is frequently worth acknowledging this. 'One's experience,' you might say, 'will influence the view one takes of this subject'. Or you might point out that 'If one assumes A, one will be more disposed to support the line taken in this answer than if one assumes B.' To do so shows not only that you know what you think and can support your views, but also that you are to some extent aware of the underlying assumptions upon which your views are based. It shows that you have achieved a considerable measure of objectivity.

Assignment D

Using the Advocate Approach, answer ONE of the following questions in not more than 1000 words:

1 'Equality is just another word for uniformity.' Do you agree?
2 To what extent is politics 'the art of the possible'?
3 'The function of a comedy is to make the audience laugh.' Discuss.
4 'All profit is theft.' Would you agree?
5 'Patriotism is the last refuge of a scoundrel'. (Dr Johnson) Discuss.
6 'This hurts me more than it hurts you!' Is it more harmful to give punishment than to receive it?
7 'Euthanasia is morally wrong.' To what extent do you support this view?
8 'It is always right to tell the truth.' Is it?

Remember to define the terms you use
Remember to ask yourself questions and to jot them down
Remember how to construct persuasive paragraphs

Once you have started writing the actual answer, allow yourself no more than two hours. Tell your tutor the exact time taken.

6. Style and tone

Summary
The following points are covered: (Fill in the page numbers
as an aid to revision.)

Page

Style

1 Use impersonal forms, not the first person 'I' — — —
2 Avoid jargon and cliché. — — —
3 Watch for overtones of approval or disapproval. — — —
4 Use phrases, not clauses, whenever possible. — — —
5 Use meaningful verbs. — — —

Tone

Tone means *your attitude towards your reader.*

1 Adopt a positive attitude towards him. — — —
2 Address him with courtesy and consideration. — — —
3 Be brief. — — —
4 *Allude* to your evidence: don't *describe* it. — — —
5 Address your reader as an equal, but with respect. — — —

6.1 Introduction

Earlier units have dealt in detail with the main structural problems to be tackled
in answering those examination questions which require a judgement to be made.
In this unit, certain points of style are considered; there is also a small section
devoted to another important matter – tone.

Neither subject is treated exhaustively. In a book of this size there is not
sufficient space to do so. Nonetheless, it seems worthwhile to give a few hints
which should help you to avoid the most common and easy-to-commit errors.

6.2 Style
6.2.1 Use of the personal pronoun 'I'

Unless you are specifically asked to give your own view, it is probably wise to
avoid the use of the first person in your answers. To write 'I think', 'I do not
agree', 'I feel' and so on is generally regarded as the intrusion of a subjective note
into what should be an objective answer. Examiners tend to prefer an impersonal
approach.

But in many questions you are asked whether you agree with a statement, or
to what extent something is true: and you must give a personal judgement. In

what form should you do it?

By and large, use impersonal forms, such as:

It seems . . . .
It would appear . . .
One might say . . .
It could be argued . . .
It is safe to assume . . .

These are all acceptable ways of indicating that you are giving an opinion, without bringing yourself into the picture to any great extent.

Self-Assessment Questions

Re-write the following passage in an impersonal form:

> **I would call Wagner a subjective artist. What I mean is that his art had its source in his personality; his work was virtually independent, I always feel, of the epoch in which he lived.**
>
> **On the other hand, I always consider Bach an objective artist. You can see that he worked only with the forms and ideas that his time proffered him. I do not think he felt any inner compulsion to open out new paths.**

Discussion

Here is a possible way of re-writing the passage:

> *Wagner was what might be called a subjective artist in that his art had its source in his personality. His work seems virtually independent of the epoch in which he lived.*
>
> *On the other hand, one can think of Bach as an objective artist. He seems to have worked only with the forms and ideas that his time proffered him, feeling no inner compulsion to open out new paths. (Adapted from J S Bach by Albert Schweitzer)*

You may have adapted the passage differently. The main point, however, is to get rid of the personal pronoun, 'I', which intrudes your opinions too strongly into a reasoned discussion of the subject.

6.2.2 Jargon

Try to avoid the use of jargon, cliche, trendy expressions, set phrases and the like. Being over-used, their meanings have become imprecise. Here is an example of jargon:

> All personnel functioning in the capacity of clerical officers should indicate to their supervisors that they have had the opportunity to take due cognizance of this notice by transmitting an acknowledgement of receipt of same.

Put simply, this merely means:

All clerks should let their supervisors know that they have seen this notice.

In the first form, there is danger of the message being lost in a welter of words. The individual words are unnecessarily long, and the writer seems to be trying to impress the clerks with his own cleverness. The second form conveys the message simply and clearly.

Self-Assessment Questions
Try to rid this passage of jargon:

The statutes covering education grant parental choice of schools so long as accommodation is available. Unfortunately, over a period of time, the schools in this Borough, because of the highly residential area and increasing housing development, have experienced difficulties with accommodation and steps have been taken to alleviate pressures on schools. Nevertheless the demand for places at present exceeds the number of places available necessitating the adherence to pupils being admitted to the schools serving their area of residence or where an elder brother or sister is already in attendance at the school chosen by the parent.

Discussion
Phrases like 'parental choice', 'residential area', 'housing developments', 'in attendance', and words like 'statutes', 'accommodation', 'alleviate', 'available', 'admitted' trip fluently from the tongues of civil servants. Such words and phrases sound impressive but mean little.
The following passage tells the parent what he needs to know, without jargon.

Parents have the right to choose their children's school so long as there is room. Unfortunately over some years pressure on school places has increased greatly because of the number of new houses built: so much so, in fact, that pupils can now only be accepted by a school if they live near it or have a brother or sister already at it.

6.2.3 Overtones
Some words tend to be shrouded in overtones so that they trigger off in the reader emotional responses over and above their actual meanings. Here are a few examples of words which, although they have a precise meaning, have come to be used more because of their emotional appeal than because of their true meaning. The first group trigger off positive responses: their users intend you to be influenced favourably by them. The second lot are intended to trigger off negative responses.

Words with overtones of approval	Words with overtones of disapproval
flexible	rigid
sophisticated	escalation
stimulating	bureaucratic
challenging	monolithic
educational	authoritarian
commitment	
imaginative	
professional	

Let us look at one of these words closely: 'challenging'. If a job is 'challenging' it presumably challenges you to use all your wits and strength. 'Challenging' has thus come to have the opposite meaning to boring. Employers advertise jobs as 'challenging' in order to attract people who like to get their teeth into something in the hope that they will get high job-satisfaction. Both employer and employee tend to assume that a 'challenging' job is a good job. The word has gained an aura of approval.

It can, however, be overdone. If every job is described as 'challenging', people will become more wary. They will realize that it is merely a euphemism for difficult and possibly underpaid jobs which they will thus avoid.

Always think twice before using an over-used word. Don't use it, in fact, if you are merely trying to convey approval. If you must use it, define the exact sense in which you intend it. Remember that you are writing for a discriminating reader – the examiner – who has almost certainly been trained to avoid jargon and cliche and to be very precise in his choice of words.

Self-Assessment Question

The following words are frequently used as much for their overtones as for their dictionary meanings:

aggressive, articulate, assertive, chronic, compromise, confront, consultation, defensive, discriminate, dogma, educational, feed-back, formal, hierarchy, immigrant, informal, inimitable, manipulative, middle-class, monitor, motivation, negative, open-ended, sensitive, supportive, systematic, therapeutic, typical, viable, work-ethic, working-class.

Arrange them in three columns to show:

Words with overtones of approval	Words with overtones of disapproval	Words whose overtones depend largely upon the user's views and opinions, or upon the context

Discussion
By their very nature, the overtones of words are imprecise. Quite likely you will disagree with some of the following placings. The point to note is that some words mean different things to different people. They must therefore be defined carefully whenever used.

Words with overtones of approval	Words with overtones of disapproval	Words whose overtones depend upon the user's views and opinions, or upon the context
articulate	aggressive	compromise
assertive	chronic	context
consultation	dogma	defensive
educational	formal	immigrant
feed-back	hierarchy	middle-class
informal	manipulative	negative
inimitable	typical	sensitive
monitor		work-ethic
motivation		working-class
open-ended		discriminate
supportive		
systematic		
therapeutic		
viable		

6.2.4 Dependent clauses

Particularly in analytical writing, one tends to use long, involved sentences. One is expressing complex ideas and one's style becomes correspondingly complex.

Try not to let your sentence ramble too wildly! One method of pruning is to cut down the number of dependent clauses (containing finite verbs), substituting phrases (governed by infinitive and participles) in their place. Look at the following sentence:

> The standard of living *which was already higher in America than in England* continued to rise because people were able to use large scale machinery *which was economical on the prairies but would have been uneconomical in the small English fields.*

This is perfectly correct gramatically, but can make its point more swiftly if well pruned. The two relative clauses, shown in italics, can be shortened into phrases:

> The standard of living, *already higher in America than in England,* continued to rise through the use of large-scale machinery, *economical on the prairies but not in small English fields.*

69

Always have an eye to brevity. You should have a lot of points to make, examples to give and ideas to express. Develop as taut a style as possible, so as to get everything down in the short time available.

Self-Assessment Questions
Underline the finite verbs in the following sentences. Reduce the number of finite verbs whenever possible.

1 **Non-professionals try to control the conditions in which they work as much as possible and in this respect they are like professionals who have perhaps had more influence in such matters when they have been discussed in the past.**

2 **Shakespeare, who was writing in the early seventeenth century, used few of the personifications which were common in the Miracle plays with which he must have been familiar.**

Discussion
The finite verbs are: 1) try, work, are, have had, have been discussed; 2) was writing, used, were, must have been.

Here are shortened versions of both sentences:

1 *Non-professionals try to control their working conditions as much as possible, just like the hitherto more influential professionals.*

2 *Shakespeare, writing in the early seventeenth century, used few of the per-sonifications common in the Miracle plays, familiar to him no doubt.*

You may feel that both sentences have been too much compressed. Even so, they illustrate the point – that you need to develop a fairly taut style of writing.

6.2.5 Meaningful verbs
The last error of style to be dealt with involves the use of verbs. The verbs 'to be' or 'to have' are over-used in analytical writing. Two examples from the American space-program illustrate this:

'We have touch-down' means 'We have touched down.'
'We have deployment of drogues' means 'The parachutes have opened.'

In both cases a static situation – 'touch-down' or 'deployment of drogues' is said to exist: 'We have a certain situation.' Put differently, one could say that *nouns* are being used for *verbs*. Nothing seems to happen and this lack of action bores the reader.

Try to use meaningful verbs, each with a distinct meaning. Whenever you are tempted to write

'They are in a class-contact situation,'

ask yourself whether you really mean

'They *are being taught*'.

And if you do, say so!

Again, if you feel like writing

At the conclusion there is a resolution of the conflict.

ask yourself whether

The conflict *is resolved* at the end.'

would be more appropriate. And if so, write it. The verbs of both second versions (italicised) pack more punch than those of the first versions.

Self-Assessment Questions
Underline the verbs used in each of the following sentences. Then improve the sentences by using more meaningful verbs:

1 The purchase of equipment was the responsibility of the Council.
2 New ideas have a good chance of implementation if there is a corresponding provision of support materials.
3 There is wide-spread recognition by teachers of the fact of their considerable influence over their pupils.
4 The Redwood City and Culver City programs were espousing diametrically opposed approaches to initial reading instruction.

Discussion
The verbs are as follows: (i) was (ii) have, is, (iii) is (iv) were espousing. The following sentences mean the same as those above, but are expressed in a more vigorous manner: notice the verbs used (underlined).

1 The Council undertook to purchase the equipment.
2 New ideas will probably be implemented if support materials are provided.
3 Many teachers recognise that they influence their pupils considerably.
4 Redwood City and Culver City taught reading differently.

6.3 Tone
By 'tone' is meant your attitude to your reader.

If you tell someone 'I do not like the tone of that remark', you imply that you detect an aggressive, scornful, facetious or derogatory attitude which, regardless of the content of the remark, you find unpleasant.

You should adopt a positive attitude towards the examiner. You should treat him courteously and considerately. The more you take account of his likely sensitivities, knowledge and requirements, the more appropriate will be the tone of your answer.

Let us look at two or three faults of tone. On the most basic level, if your hand-writing is poor the examiner is likely to be put off. 'This candidate,' he will think, 'does not appear to mind whether or not I can read what he writes. It cannot therefore be very important.' So always write as clearly and set out your work as neatly as you can.

Another mistake it is all too easy to make is to bore your reader. Try not to be a bore! A bore tells you *everything*, whether you already know it or not. If writing, for example, about strategy in the Second World War, do not say that Churchill broadcast to the British people:

'Never before in the history of human endeavour was so much owed by so many to so few.'

The examiner surely knows this; or, at any rate, he ought to know it. Try instead, to allude to the speech with some such words as

Churchill's tribute to 'the few' stressed the dependence of the country on its first line of defence, the RAF fighter pilots.

This remark is designed not to tell the examiner what he already knows, but to make the point that the country's protection depended on its pilots.

Try always to consider what it is reasonable to expect your reader to know, and write accordingly. By this means you will maintain his interest.

Finally, there is the question of what you might call the level from which you address your reader. Should you talk down to him? Should you address him on equal terms? Or should you speak to him as to a superior being?

By and large, address him as an equal. You are trying to persuade him to accept your point of view by means of rational argument. The fact that you reason with someone implies that you are treating him as an equal. You probably adopt this tone with your friends. To people whom you consider inferior or superior to you (if such people exist!) you might use a different tone — dogmatic or subservient, as the case might be.

The table shows the sort of phrases which characterise the different tones of address: (The phrases illustrating 'talking down' and 'subservient' are somewhat exaggerated!)

Attitude to your reader	Characteristics	Typical phrases
Talking down to him	God-like omniscience Unduly forceful Didactic Dogmatic	'You must understand. . .' '. . .no question but that. .' 'Undoubtedly. . .' And if you believe that, you will believe. . .'

Attitude to your reader	Characteristics	Typical phrases
On an equal footing with him	Good manners Consideration for your reader Civilised conversation	'It is reasonable to assume. . .' 'It would be unwise to pay too much attention to. . .' 'It may be recalled that. .' 'It is, perhaps, an over-statement to suggest that. . .' 'It seems . . .' 'It appears that. . .'
Subservient towards him	Obsequious The 'Uriah Heep' approach Unduly diffident	'If I might make so bold as to suggest. . .' 'My humble opinion, for what it's worth. . .' 'I offer this view for your esteemed consideration. . .'

Assignment E

Develop *five* of the topic sentences listed below into paragraphs. Follow the Paragraph Plan of Unit 3 as closely as possible, inserting numbers (1, 2, 3a, 3b, 4) to show the different parts.

Don't forget that in this assignment you are not aiming to give a balanced view of the topics set, but merely to develop each idea as clearly and strongly as you can.

Concentrate on achieving a good style and on using an appropriate tone, as discussed in the unit you have just read.

1 Our motives are not always as altruistic as we think them.
2 It is easy to over-estimate one's own merits.
3 For most people, sympathetic surroundings are necessary for happiness.
4 Some people seem happy in spite of their surroundings.
5 Fear of public opinion stunts individual growth.
6 There is no point in deliberately flouting public opinion.
7 Applied science has enormously increased the world's population.
8 Cultivated people are a drop of ink in the ocean.
9 A sense of personal morality cannot be developed by simply laying down the law.
10 It is hard for one generation to understand another.
11 'Merrie England' must have been a strange place.
12 We tend to regard life in the open air idealistically.

13   We have lost something by living closely packed in cities and towns.

14   Fishing has always been a popular pastime.

Send your five paragraphs to your tutor.

7. Translating theory into practice

Who ever thinks a faultless piece to see,
Thinks what ne'er was, nor is, nor e'er shall be.

Pope

This is really a revision unit. You have been offered plenty of advice on different aspects of the central problem — how to answer questions where you are asked to make a judgement. Now let us check to see whether you have understood the advice.

Here is a candidate's answer to the question:

'English schools perform well their job of educating the young.' Discuss.

The candidate has tried to follow the advice given in the book. He has, however, departed on occasions from a literal interpretation of it. Not every paragraph follows the Paragraph Plan, for example. But, by and large, he has presented his answer fairly well.

Opposite the candidate's answer, you will find an analysis of it.

1 Read the candidate's answer right through without looking at the analysis.
2 Re-read the answer, paragraph by paragraph, and then jot down what you think are its main features
3 After each paragraph, compare what you have written with the analysis given.

MODEL ANSWER

'English schools perform well their job of educating the young.' Discuss.

1 Though certain reservations need to be made, the somewhat vague remark quoted above gives a fair picture of the work of English schools today.

2 The remark is vague in so far as it leaves undefined what is meant by 'educating the young'. To make this more precise is to enter a battlefield fought over by innumerable armies, each with their own ideas of what schools should and should not provide for their pupils. Nonetheless, some attempt at definition must be made, and perhaps the best starting point is to look at what seems to be the central controversy: namely, should the development of individuality on the one hand, or the socialising of the individual on the other, have precedence?

3 Almost all teachers and almost all schools attempt some sort of balance between these conflicting aims of education. And as a very rough generalisation — and in spite of all the attacks made on schools for failing in their function — it seems fair to say that they achieve both aims with a modest measure of success. The reservation, noted at the outset, which needs to be made, is that English schools seem less effective than they might be at allowing individuality to flourish. Let us now look at this relative failure in some detail.

4 Particularly in the sort of plural society which exists today, with many different possible ways of earning a living, many different possible 'life-styles' and many different value systems, there is a need for each person to be independent and adaptable and to gain a broad view of life and of the world. To achieve the ideal of breadth of vision, one would think that the curriculum should span as wide a range of subjects as is compatible with serious study — not mere tasting. To achieve the ideal of independence and adaptability, students should be able to choose, within reasonable limits, what subjects to study and which parts of each subjects to concentrate upon. Self-programming, not routine, should be the order of the day. English schools seem to fall considerably short of both ideals: the curriculum tends to be narrow, and there is too much routine.

ANALYSIS OF MODEL ANSWER

'English schools perform well their job of educating the young. Discuss.

Paragraph 1. The lack of precision in the question has forced the candidate to devote the first three or four paragraphs to defining the subject and stating his position. He has noted the need for a strong opening remark: he gives his own view at the very beginning.

The Advocate Approach has been adopted. Verdict Two has been used: 'There is a considerable truth in the statement.' The words 'somewhat vague' have been used to give a link with the next paragraph in which 'education' is to be defined.

Paragraph 2. Definition of the purpose of education is notoriously difficult. The candidate felt that this should be pointed out so that the examiner could not criticise him for over-simplification. The candidate has eventually chosen to look at what he considers the central issue — should schools produce people to fill jobs or should they develop personality for its own sake? To deal with central issues is wise. In a large subject, concentrate your energies on essentials, even at the risk of over-simplification.

Paragraph 3. The candidate gives his reservation against complete agreement with the statement. He shows how English schools might perform better by allowing individuality to flourish rather more.

Paragraph 4. The 'relative failure' is examined in more detail. The candidate sets up an ideal educational system and indicates how it might be achieved. He says that English schools do not live up to this ideal, and he isolates two particular faults — narrowness and routine — each fault being the opposite of his ideal. (One could perhaps criticise him for his choice of 'routine' as the opposite of 'independence and adaptability').

5 That the curriculum of some English schools is narrow, may be seen in the scant emphasis placed on the visual arts or design; in the comparatively small development of individual musical talent; in the lack of systematic help given to pupils to pursue outside interests; and more generally, in the reluctance to pay more than lip service to what cannot be measured in terms of examination successes.

6 (a) But the charge of narrowness can best perhaps be substantiated by a glance at the system of A-level examinations. (b) At an age when young people should be extending their horizons to gain a wide view of the world and of human achievements, they are faced with the need to concentrate on two or three subjects to the exclusion of all others. (c) All too frequently, a sixth-form student will narrow his field of study to either the arts or the sciences. (d) It is hard for him at a later stage to bridge what C P Snow has called the 'two-culture' gap, having been encouraged to think of these two cultures as mutually exclusive. (e) Admittedly, schools have tried, by introducing 'minority-time' subjects, to widen the sixth-form curriculum; and pressure is building up from the Schools Council to introduce a five-subject norm for sixth-formers (N- and F -levels). (f) But at present, the curriculum for the adolescent seems unduly restrictive.

7 (a) To turn to the charge of too much routine, one can illustrate this from all levels of school life. (b) In many subjects, pages of exercises are the order of the day; French verbs and history dates must be learned by rote, innumerable quadratic equations solved, complex sentences analysed, mortise and tenon joints sawed and chiselled, notes on science copied from the blackboard. (c) Curiosity would seem stifled by such hum-drum work – as can be seen by the high proportion of pupils who shake the dust of school off their feet at the earliest possible moment, never to study seriously or even to open a book again. (d) 'All work and no play makes Jack a dull boy' has more than a ring of truth in this connection.

8 (a) Having looked then, perhaps somewhat harshly, at certain shortcomings of English schools in developing individuality, we turn to their brighter aspects. (b) Here, it must be admitted that by and large they make a good job of training their pupils in the qualities needed for earning a living and taking part in the workings of society. (c) At their best, they teach the virtue of hard work. (d) In the infant school, pupils are praised for the effort they put into the tasks set; in secondary schools, good work earns promotion to higher sets or classes; and the carrots of future rewards – university entry or secure jobs – are continually dangled before the noses of O-level and A-level candidates. (c) Those pupils able enough to compete in the external examination hurdle race

Paragraph 5. The charge of narrowness is briefly illustrated by three specific examples (art, music and outside interests) and by one generalisation (examination success). This paragraph really leads up to the next one where the charge is more strongly substantiated.

Paragraph 6. (a) The candidate has attempted to prove the charge of narrowness beyond all reasonable doubt. (b) he contrasts his ideal (breadth of vision) with the actual (specialisation) (c & d) He shows how this leads to a division between arts and the sciences. (e) He shows that he is not the only person to take this view, citing the Schools Council in support. (f) But he re-inforces his charge of narrowness by saying that hoped-for changes have not yet occurred.

Paragraph 7. (a) 'To turn to'. . . acts as a link. The candidate wants to discuss a different topic and shows the examiner that he will change to a different tack. (b) He illustrates the charge of too much routine by choosing courses at many different levels in schools to counter any possible accusation of looking only at A- level courses. (c) He cites the ex-pupils who 'vote with their feet' by never studying again as evidence that his charge is correct. (d) He generalises by quoting a nursery rhyme.

Paragraph 8. (a) The candidate uses a link-sentence to summarise what has gone before (criticism of schools) and to introduce his main contention (b) that English schools are good in the way they fit their pupils for later life. (c) This is the topic sentence, which concerns the virtue of hard work. (d) Three examples are given from the entire school age range (5 − 18). (e) He states the topic sentence more fully. (f) He stresses the importance of the realisation that progress can be made by one's efforts.

come to realize that success in many fields is gained by working to overcome the problems which present themselves. (f) And this is an important insight to learn.

9 (a) Another quality needed for earning one's living in an interesting way is the ability to delve deep into a subject, not merely to skim over its surface. And here again English schools do well. (b) For it must be acknowledged that the very narrowness of the sixth-form curriculum criticised above actually encourages study in depth. (c) In studying the history of the First World War, for example, the student may be presented with official accounts written by both sides and asked to explain discrepancies. (d) This may lead him to consider whether any truly 'objective' account — free of bias of any kind — can ever be given of, say, a battle; or for that matter, of any other historical event. (e) He will thus be encouraged to probe the surface of mere facts to philosophical issues which lie beneath. (f) In a similar manner, the study of character in a play by Molière may have psychological ramifications for the A-level French student, and the study of Ancient History may have sociological ones. (g) In each case, the student is led to realise that in the last resort he must make up his own mind on issues: appeal to authority is of no avail where authorities conflict. (h) This realisation is of inestimable value for someone whose life will require him to take from time to time a difficult decision, the outcome of which will be uncertain.

10 Two or three further aspects of training pupils to fit into society may be mentioned in passing. English schools teach with passable success the need to work together. Teamwork is perhaps an unfashionable word to use in this respect, but the value of mutual cooperation which it implies is instilled through games, orchestras, bands, and inter-house competitions of various kinds. Also the need for discipline, punctuality and orderliness is impressed, perhaps over-strongly, by a welter of proscriptive rules and sanctions — no-talking rules, no-running rules and no-fighting rules, to name but a few. And English schools are perhaps unique in giving a taste of responsibility to older pupils for certain aspects of running the institution. In all these ways, by setting themselves up as it were as a microscosm of society, English schools help to socialise their pupils.

11 In judging how well schools do their job, providing that certain minimum standards are met, one is really considering the balance between different values. As has been pointed out earlier, English schools err if anything on the socialising side, to the relative detriment of individual creativeness. In America, the balance is different: there, individuality is given pre-eminence and standards of achievement suffer. In France, on the contrary, even more value than in England is attached to the learning of facts, little concession

Paragraph 9. This paragraph follows closely the Paragraph Plan set out in Unit 3. The controlling idea is that English schools encourage their pupils to delve deep into a topic, not merely skim its surface. (a) The phrase 'Another quality needed for earning one's living in an interesting way' acts as a link with the previous paragraph. The rest of the sentence is really the topic sentence. (b) The candidate pins down the reason for success – the narrowness which he has previously argued against. So as not to be criticised too heavily for taking both sides at once (for and against 'narrowness'), he tells the examiner what he is doing in the phrase 'For it must be acknowledged. . .'. To point out the weakness of one's own argument disarms a critic. You destroy the sharpness of his attack. (c, d & e) These three sentences give one example in some detail. (f) Two other examples are touched upon in this sentence. (g) & (h) The candidate returns directly to the controlling idea, mentioning the value of delving deep.

Paragraph 10. The candidate gives the examiner three other examples of the success of English schools in educating the young. (Remember that this success is his main contention: he must make a strong case in favour of it, so as to outweigh the reservations made earlier). Had he had time, he could have developed each example into a separate paragraph.

Paragraph 11. The candidate has ended by trying to place the achievement of English schools beside that of the schools of other countries. He has chosen American and French schools, because these provide a neat contrast, the first differing in one way, the second in another. In the final sentence he has tried, perhaps not very successfully, to account for the differences.

being made to differences between schools, let alone between individuals. Perhaps the English love of pragmatism as opposed to theory, and of an orderly society as opposed to a more violent one, has contributed to its schools striking the balance where they do.

8.Examinations

Examinations test both knowledge and skill. Knowledge comes from wide and deep reading, from lectures and from discussions. Skill is developed by constant practice in writing such as this book has aimed to give.

In an examination, you must work within very stringent constraints, the main one being the time-limit. Other constraints are the need to stick to the points, to define your terms, and to back up your opinions with evidence.

Examinations are not exercises in free expression. Reams of waffle, padding, verbiage − call it what you will − are quite out of place. What you must aim for is an answer which shows that you know your subject and can express your views succinctly.

So always be utterly business-like: plan your answer paper as a whole, and plan your time carefully. Let us look at each of these in turn.

First, here are some general points about planning your answer paper as a whole.

1 *Read the rubric* (ie. the instructions). Do exactly what you are told to do.
2 *Answer the right number of questions* − neither more nor less. You gain no marks for answering extra questions. And you give yourself a *severe handicap* by not answering enough questions.
3 *Choose the questions carefully* − read the whole question paper through. Strike out questions you cannot answer. But do not strike them out too quickly. Sometimes a question which looks stiff on the face of things appears easier after a little thought.
4 *Answer the easiest question first.* This will boost your confidence. When you come to the question you find most difficult, remember that it is not too hard to gain the first 50% of the marks, however shaky your knowledge; you will make a good impression by analysing the question thoroughly and stating your views clearly.
5 *Plan your answer.* Underline the key concepts in the question.
   Jot down: (a) your own questions about these key concepts
             (b) any ideas you feel appropriate to the answer
             (c) examples which will help to prove your point.
   Think hard about the question: worry it, like a dog at a bone. Keep jotting your ideas down.
   Arrange your jottings in an appropriate order.
6 *Then write out your answer.* (Write the question at the top of your sheet of paper. Refer to it every now and then to check that you are keeping to the point.) Write your answer systematically, with reasonable speed. Don't rush. Write clearly − you will not have time to copy your answer out again.
7 *Avoid 'the prepared answer.'* Never try to recall the answer you did for home-

work a week or two ago. Answer the question set, not the question you would have liked to be set, nor yet the question your teacher told you might be set. However closely these may resemble the question set, they are unlikely to be exactly the same.

The 'prepared answer' is one of the major bugbears of examiners!

We have looked at general points to be aware of in planning your answer. Now, let us consider how to make best use of the limited time available to you in the examination.

1 Have your watch on your desk in front of you. You will need to refer to it frequently.

2 Divide the total time allowed for the whole paper equally between the questions. Write down the exact times when each new answer should be started.

3 Allow 5–10 minutes for planning each answer. Make sure that you start writing out your answer before your 10 minutes planning time has elapsed.

4 10 minutes before the end of each answer, if you have much more material, make your remaining points as briefly as possible. 5 minutes before the end of each answer, start writing your concluding paragraph.

5 Finish each answer on the dot. DO NOT OVER-RUN.

6 Allow 10 minutes at the end of the paper to re-read, correct spelling, grammar, syntax, style, etc.

7 Never leave the examination room before the end of the time allotted.

In general, resist all inclination to panic! However hard the questions may seem, remember that you can produce a good answer if you remain cool.

So, NOT Good Luck, BUT Good Management!

Assignment F

And so each venture
Is a new beginning, a raid on the inarticulate.
T S Eliot
There is no substitute for continual practice in writing if you want to improve your performance. In view of this, the final assignment is to write an answer to one of the questions below.

Answer it as nearly under examination conditions as possible: From the time you have chosen which question to answer, allow yourself *1½ hours only*, including 10 minutes for your plan and 5 minutes to read through. Try not to have any interruption during the 1½ hours.

REMEMBER — Get to the point
— Define your terms

- Make yourself clear
- Be persuasive
- See that you back up your points with evidence
- Keep to the point
- ANSWER THE QUESTION

(i) 'The majority is always wrong.' Discuss.

(ii) 'It is better to have *any* religion than none at all.' Discuss.

(iii) 'The annual party conferences in Britain are of little value to the parties themselves or to the general public.' Discuss.

(iv) 'Pop festivals are among the more anti-social activities of our times.' Examine this view.

(v) 'A high standard of living does not necessarily mean a more cultured society.' Consider this statement.

(vi) 'Advertising succeeds in selling goods at the cost of human values.' Do you agree?

Send your Assignment to your tutor with a note of the exact time taken.

COURSE COMMENTS

Please send your comments on this course to Courses Editor, NEC, 18 Brooklands Avenue, Cambridge CB2 2HN

Name . . . .

Student No. . . . .

Address . . . .

. . . .

. . . .

(ED14)